Losing Kali

Kali Rae Wheeler

Copyright 2017 © Kali Rae Wheeler

All rights reserved. No part of this book may be reproduced in any form or by any electronic or mechanical means, including information storage and retrieval systems, without written permission from the author, except in the case of a reviewer, who may quote brief passages embodied in critical articles or in a review.

Trademarked names appear throughout this book. Rather than use a trademark symbol with every occurrence of a trademarked name, names are used in an editorial fashion, with no intention of infringement of the respective owner's trademark.

The information in this book is distributed on an "as is" basis, without warranty. Although every precaution has been taken in the preparation of this work, neither the author nor the publisher shall have any liability to any person or entity with respect to any loss or damage caused or alleged to be caused directly or indirectly by the information contained in this book.

I have tried to recreate events, locales and conversations from my memories of them. In order to maintain their anonymity in some instances I have changed the names of individuals and places, I may have changed some identifying characteristics and details such as physical properties, occupations and places of residence.

ISBN: 978-1-62967-086-7 (Paperback)
ISBN: 978-1-62967-087-4 (Hardcover)
Library of Congress Control Number: 2017930021

Dedication

This book is dedicated to the people either struggling with a mental disorder, or struggling with a pseudo-mental disorder fueled by Big Pharma, abuse, or trauma, anyone who's ever been a victim of sexual assault or sexual misconduct in the workplace and any soul who's been struck by the increase in mass shootings around the nation and our world.

We are all in this together.

Love and light to you. XO, Kali Rae

Contents

Preface	i
Thank You	iii
Introduction: A Good Kid Overview	v
Author's Note	vii
A Letter Home	xi
Abbreviations and Terms	xiii
List of Doctors	xv
Part I: Middle School	1
My Sister Got Drunk; I Got A Therapist	2
Locker Assignments, New Friends, and Queenie	6
Protected	8
Walking the Mile	10
A Good Kid	13
One Girl's Strength	15
Hanging with Z-Boys: I Thought I Was Penny Lane	17
The One Provision	20
The Quintessential Sk8r Boi	26
Part II: Freshman Year	29
Aruba: Setting Goals	30
Our Town's Tony Robbins	33
A Summer Affair: Gnarls Barkley	35
The Prozac Experience	44
Dr. Hollenberg's Advice	55
Part III: Sophomore Year	57
The Index Card	58
Mononucleosis: I Can't Stop	61
Dr. Whittman's Trick	65
My Doctor's Communicated!...Not!	70
Meeting Nurse Ratched: The Portofino Rehab Center	71
Abridged for the Reader's Health	74

The Portofino Journal	75
A Doggy Bag of Prescription Samples and a Hawaiian T-Shirt	91
Reflections on Meeting Dr. Morano	94
Unknown Number	96
The Boys' Dance, Keg-Stands, and Choices	97
Spring Break: Palm Desert with the Terpsichore Girls	103
Dose Switching in May	106
Sixteen Candles, a Goldfish, and a Range Rover	108
Seroquel'd in Public, More Specifically, in Maui	111
Dr. Morano Goes iRobot	114
Prom: A Night to Forget	116
Blaise's Guest House: Things Speed Up	119
It Didn't Hurt Me	123
An Enlightening Urgent Care Visit	126
Repercussions: The Leather Journal	128
Part IV: Junior Year	**137**
Dr. Fiaschetti's Encyclopedia of Medications	138
An Internship in the Hills	140
More Diagnosis, Fewer Answers	144
Cruel Humor and Witnessing Terror in a Bystander	145
He Almost Drove Me Home	154
The Things People Notice	158
Jay Gatsby: Jaxx Moreau	159
The Flower Streets	162
Bayside Restaurant	168
Gatsby Saves the Day with Denim	170
New Years with Jaxx and the Beach Crew	172
The Portofino Journal Revisited	175
Jimi Hendrix and The Intruders: Pre Court Rituals	176
"Inappropriately Sexual": Disagreements with Mom	182
Dinners with Gatsby	185
Driving into Compton: Witnessing my First Drug Deal	189
Three Bars	194
Dr. Morano's Mental Break: My Psychiatrist Was Tased	196
Let's See About Tomorrow: The New Journal	202

Grandpa Weber's Famous Infinity Pool ... 203
Poetry & Prescriptions: The Leather Journal ... 207

Part V: Senior Year ... **211**
Groundhog's Day: Let's Try Something—The Same? ... 213
The Text ... 214
A Letter to the Lost ... 219
First Real Attempt ... 221
October 08, 2008 ... 223
The Thirteenth Stepper ... 225
The Gift That Keeps on Giving: Topamax's Kidney Stones ... 229
A Trip to Arrowhead Turns into a Trip to See Cathy ... 231
Uneven Ground: The Leather Journal ... 239
Waiting for the Suboxone Delivery ... 242
The Debutante Ball ... 243
Under the Lights: Valedictorian Speech ... 245

Epilogue: My Doctors are Famous ... **247**
Dr. Cathy on Prime-Time News ... 248
Dr. Morano Close Behind ... 249
Retrieving the Medical Records ... 251
Mother Knew Best All Along ... 254

Afterword ... **255**

Appendices ... **257**
Appendix A ... 258
Appendix B ... 260
Appendix C ... 261
Appendix D ... 264
Appendix E ... 267
Appendix F ... 270
Appendix G ... 272
Appendix H ... 274
Appendix I ... 276
Appendix J ... 277
Appendix K ... 278
Appendix L ... 280
Appendix M ... 281

Appendix N	283
Appendix O	284
Appendix P	285
Appendix Q	286
Appendix R	287
Appendix S	288
Glossary of Useful Terms	**291**
References	**293**
Thank You	**299**

Preface

Seven years from the time my pharmaceutical hell commenced, I found myself in a frenzied search for answers. I was past the point of realizing what had happened to me and was now out for justice. It was time to become the detective of my past and place the pieces of this catastrophic jigsaw puzzle back together. I needed to collect information outside of my experiences. I found myself reeling from the pain surfacing from all the self-excavation. I needed the inspiration to press forward; to continue past how much I wanted to pull my hair out and burn the doctor's records.

I found a few documentaries while working late night in the recording studio, which provided a spark of perseverance and the validity to continue climbing the mountain toward the summit. A clear pattern was emerging; the things that I experienced were not unique to me, they were plaguing the nation, even if it was behind closed doors. There was a real bad ass monster that I needed to slay for the rest of us. One documentary, in particular, *Boy Interrupted* (Perry 2009), clarified a critical concept and emblazoned it into my mind.

The documentary is about a teenage boy who suffered from bipolar disorder. He showed signs as early as two years old. He had dramatic mood swings where he said violent things. He would isolate himself. He would throw tantrums. All the typical mental illness checkmarks were there. He was also very well-liked and had many friends.

After weaning himself off of his prescriptions due to their adverse side effects; feeling tired, numb, headachy, etc., that he had reportedly (by parents, teachers, and friends) been doing so well on, he tragically took his own life.

What shook me to the core was what he had written on his laptop just moments before. He wrote of the universal emotions that plague the process of growing up. They were emotions that I had documented clearly, but more importantly, remembered clearly, and felt so profoundly. The catch is that I reported feeling these things more powerfully while under the influence of psychotropic drugs.

My lack of self-awareness and the inability to control impulses came out of thin air. I may have felt the same things no matter what, but when I was on the drugs, the desire to act was tangible. Many times I felt like I was being drawn to the edge of the cliff or taunted by the pill bottle to take more. I can still, to this day, remember the unmistakable surge of adrenaline that accompanied these feelings. It was animalistic: the feeling similar to sprinting the last quarter-mile of a 5k marathon using some strength and speed I never knew I had.

The impulses were often so intense that I had to have my best friend Tessa babysit me, or at least stay on the phone with me until it passed. I often pondered how much time it would take to break away from whoever I was with and jump off the nearest bridge. Each time I'd have this intense drive to kill myself. But, thoughts of not being killed by the fall and rather left disabled plagued me. If I were pondering using pills, I would worry that I would end up a vegetable, which would put even more of a burden on my parents. The thoughts that held me back were the possibility that the attempt would not produce fatal results.

I'd come to find years later, that not only was the impulse to take my life made stronger, while under the influence of prescription drugs, the ideations themselves may have been a direct result of the drugs themselves.

By miracle, I am alive today to tell you that; a mentally ill, chemically imbalanced person becomes balanced when given the right chemicals and therefore, he steps back from the ledge.

A chemically stable, but emotionally unstable teenager given the same brain altering drugs becomes chemically imbalanced on top of everything else going on in a growing brain, and therefore, he or she is propelled toward the ledge. It is a biochemical equation; imbalanced, apt to jump, balanced naturally but put into a state of artificial imbalance, apt to jump. The latter is possibly even more dangerous than the former. It all depends upon the strength of the imbalance, whether it be biological or pharmaceutical, the equation doesn't change.

Thank You

Thank you to my family who stuck by me and supported me through the worst of times.

Thank you for not putting me in a mental institution when I was a nut. (Although your reasoning was that I probably would have talked my way out of it and made you guys look nuts instead...) But thank you for not calling nonetheless...haha.

Thank you, Grandma, for consistently pushing me toward my dreams and providing me with a foundation of confidence.

And thank you, Steve, for telling me that the work would always be less relevant the longer I wait to expose it. Thank you for explaining that the artist will always look back at the previous day's, month's, year's work and think it isn't good enough anymore because we learn new lessons each day. Thank you for your inspiring talks at the studio and your bone-chilling guitar riffs that got me through some of the worst of times. Much love to you and your heart of gold.

And, C. Thank you for everything. But mostly for practicing what you preach—JUST DO IT—and ever so subtly reminding me that I hadn't just done it yet.

Introduction: A Good Kid Overview

I am from a small suburban beach town, composed of Anglo-Saxon Protestant Republican extremely affluent families (the entire democratic population of our city fit inside my home).

Households in my area are composed of a few fundamental elements; two or three kids enrolled in many extracurricular activities, a father who worked late, but came home in time for dinner, a mother who attended fitness classes every morning and an expectation that each child will go to a top university and either become: A) a Doctor B) a lawyer or C) a successful entrepreneur with the financial backing of their trust fund.

I could not have asked for a more privileged, yet humble upbringing. I never thought twice about the expense of raising three children and taking them all on vacation each Christmas, ski, spring, and summer vacation. Our school district even had a "Ski Week" in February to go to the local mountains and ski.

If we didn't have a home-cooked meal each night hot and ready for all five of us, it was "Del Taco" night. It was a weekly celebration when my sister or I had to be picked up from dance class late, and needed calories for the fifteen-minute drive home back to the Coast.

In the summertime, I was a top swimmer on the local swim team. I trained twice a day on some occasions, hoping to grab the record in the County Finals where I would compete against the best swimmer on the rival team in the 50-meter butterfly. No one else in the county came close to beating either of us. I eventually won it, but only after my rival took the win in freestyle. When both sides of the community filtered into the same 7-12 school, we became best friends.

I had two older siblings show me the ropes. My brother protected and defended me at all costs. My mother was more concerned with sewing the best Annie costume, finding a club swim team and managing my sister's carpool to Arts School, than with weighing the possibilities that what a trusted doctor had prescribed her child was harmful and potentially lethal.

Right from the start, I was destined to hyper-intuitiveness and hypersensitivity to everything around me. I was born with an autoimmune disorder that caused me to be a bit more of a medical mystery than my siblings, but academically, socially, athletically, and artistically; I was gifted.

In 1st grade, I wrote a book that my classmate displayed as her favorite book on her "About Me" poster hung up on the classroom wall. In 2nd grade I started my first nonprofit campaign, organizing my papers in a metallic unicorn folder. Stamps arrived from the ASPCA after my parents' apparent contribution, and I felt I needed to do my part. I wrapped an old coffee can in construction paper and carefully crafted "Save the Whales" in bubble letters next to a colored pencil drawing of a blue whale. The next morning, I gave a speech to my class about whaling and placed the donation can in the back of the classroom.

By 3rd grade, I was in the Gifted and Talented Education Program (G.A.T.E.) and by the fourth grade, a poem I wrote in class became the talk of the teachers' lounge and the talk around our dinner table.

At the end of 1st grade, the Principal suggested I head on up to 3rd grade. I fought heavily against this idea. My friends were all in my grade. I was worried that if I skipped a grade, I would lose the friends I had had all my life. They asked again every year following. In fourth grade, I could skip two full grade levels, but once again, I fought against it. Ironically, both things unintentionally came to fruition in the years to follow.

Author's Note

In the process of writing this first book, now the first of three in *The Finding Kali* Series, I dug into every place I could imagine.

I compiled the journals that I had meticulously kept since the invention of the gel pen. I retrieved hard copies of all of my medical records from more than a dozen different sources; doctors, therapists, hospitals, and a stuffed manila envelope of all the different departments of medicine at the University I attended.

I scoured emails, class assignments from middle school all the way up until my last classes before receiving my B.A. and the scribblings in the margins of my notes from engineering school after that.

I searched obsessively through old social media outlets, not only find specific dates but to reread painful conversations and find the facts amongst all the feelings. The Facebook messages were some of the worst. I'd since deactivated that account. In reactivating it, I was able to look with a microscope at the random pilings of memories and mishaps.

I typed out each and every one of the journal entries and transcribed the medical records, keepsakes, and notes written by lovers, letters from Grandma, birthday cards: everything. I needed everything I could find, no matter how painful, so that I could to place myself exactly where I had been when things occurred.

I crafted timeline after timeline, linking the medical records and notes, cross-referencing the social media conversations, photographs, and even essays written in class to coinciding events in my life.

I sorted the array of mind jogging memories in piles by year, then meticulously by month and then even by day in some cases. I had to see things right next to one another, in physical form, to believe that these events happened the way that they did. I couldn't second guess cold hard facts.

I struggled with anger I felt toward a broken system. But also anger with myself for not doing this sooner or realizing my own worth and getting out of situations before the exit disappeared altogether. And I spent some days mad at others and at the ways we treat each other so differently on this planet even although we are all made up of the same matter.

Having placed pieces of a sometimes intentionally forgotten puzzle back in order, I held my breath and questioned family members to get a full perspective. These were not fun conversations.

I am very auditory and often remember events solely from words exchanged. I crafted dialogue from what I remembered.

Certain people are excluded from the final book to ensure that I only portray the essential characters in getting this message across to you, the reader.

All names of individuals involved have been changed to assure privacy. At certain times, specific attributes and locations have been changed to preserve the integrity of the individuals and their families.

My goal for this book has nothing to do with pinpointing certain people. That will do no good in this situation. My goal is to shed light on an issue that is plaguing us all. We are all in this together, and as one we need to come together and fix this.

I did many hours of research on the effects of pharmaceuticals on our population, pulling from articles in medical journals to discussion boards on popular medical websites, to news broadcasts and even the local newspaper.

I did not include these articles in this book to preserve the anonymity of the people involved. By directly injecting these stories, I felt it would be overstepping my bounds into a territory that I do not need to cross to tell my story.

Lastly, the Internet searches I performed to locate some of the uniquely corrupt individuals I encountered, brought about an array of incredibly scary results.

However, with much thought, I decided that these, even convicted criminals, deserve the right to privacy and held fast to the notion that this is not a book to "out" specific parties, but rather to shed light on a terrible epidemic.

What I can say is that several doctors, as well as people and situations on this harrowing journey, have, not only been brought to the of the attention of the general public, but to justice. And some of the large-scale problems I encounter have recently been the topics of news specials and in a few cases, sections of late-night comedy shows.

In order to see the beauty in something, you must stand at a distance and see it from a new angle before returning: whether that takes moments or years.

To fully immerse yourself in a message, you must let it reveal itself in its own time. If you are unable to pull yourself away, unable to hold something loosely, you will never be able to embrace it appropriately and therefore; you do not deserve its beauty. You do not recognize the work for what it is, but rather what you see in it. You are only then appreciating yourself: your perception.

If you can't let go and watch something flourish without you, you do not belong in its airspace. Once you detach, you will finally decipher the things you thought were so simple. You may unlock meanings that, until now, remained hidden from you, or new pathways that can now be treasured. You discover new reasons for being a part of this person or this message's life.

The ability to watch a piece of art draw the attention of others, to stimulate a reaction in another's mind and activate some latent memory crucial for this new person's step forward in life that is brilliance.

In this spirit, I'm stepping back and letting go in the hope that I can save someone else from going through what I went through.

Freshman year of high school, in my Honors English class, I had to write a mock letter home during wartime. I stumbled across it recently and found that it was perfect to preface the start of my high school career and this book.

So, here it is.

Namaste.

Kali Rae

A Letter Home

Dear Isaak,

It's a lot different here than I thought it would be. The war really puts things into perspective for me. Every day I see my fellow soldiers fall victim to the vicious cycle of fighting. We lie trapped in the trenches day in and day out, waiting, wondering, watching. Will I ever get out of here? The days go by slowly, but thinking of the family helps me through each day. The trenches are muddy, cold and eerie, and the rats run freely over our feet at night. They also enjoy stealing the small rations of food we are dealt. Those nasty little creatures! To pass the time I write letters, mostly to you. Some I will never send; some I will. I've become quite the artist as well. I spend at least an hour a day drawing. I usually draw pictures of places I'd rather be, of home, or of other beautiful places I'd rather be. Nonetheless I fight for you guys! I know in my heart that I will return home safely and these feelings help me through these perilous days. I never thought I would be put in a situation so eye opening, so awful. Tangible objects are nothing to me now. The only thing I hold dear is the one photograph I have of us at Christmas last year. We are all sitting by the fireplace, watching the flames engulf the cedar-scented logs. I keep that picture in my pocket, close to my heart. I can't wait to see you all again. I know it will be soon. I hope that everything at home is fine. Please do not worry too much about me. I promise you that everything will be okay.

Love you always and forever,
Kali Rae

Abbreviations and Terms

A/P	assessment/plan
Add	additional notes from the doctor or nurse to add to my file
AED	antiepileptic drug
BMI	body mass index
CT	or CAT scan, an x-ray scan of your insides
D/C	discontinue
Dx	diagnosis
F/U	follow up
GP	general practitioner
Hashimotos	an autoimmune disorder where the body attacks the thyroid gland
Hx	history
MD	medical doctor
Misc. AEDs	Depakote
Misc. Antibiotics	Cipro, Macrobid, Omnicef, Z-pack, Augmentin, amoxicillin, Bactrim
O	"objective," Dr. findings and/or results to tests done in the office
Rx	prescription
S	"subjective," information from the patient's perspective
SS	serotonin syndrome
SSRI	selective serotonin reuptake inhibitor
Synthroid	medicine I take for Hashimotos

UTI	urinary track infection, misdiagnosis, in my case, of kidney stones
W	weight

List of Doctors

Dr. Fiaschetti, MD psychiatrist

Dr. Jane, MD my original general practitioner and the mother of Dr. Scott.

Dr. Jensen, MD psychiatrist

Dr. Morano, MD general practitioner acting as a psychiatrist

Dr. Roberts, MD urgent care physician

Dr. Sandy, Ph. D psychologist

Dr. Scott, MD my general practitioner, also the son of Dr. Jane.

Dr. Thompson, MD psychiatrist

Dr. Whittman, Ph. D psychologist

Part I:
Middle School

My Sister Got Drunk; I Got A Therapist

The first time I ever went to a therapist was because of my sister. It is 2003, and I am in sixth grade.

Our family rented a room for Kayla in Palm Springs. Palm Desert is the destination for our district during spring break. Not only did our entire school, which was grades 7-12, travel to the desert for the week, the school across the Bay, Newport Beach High School, "Beach," make it their destination as well. It was free-reign for the high school kids; lots of alcohol, fellow high schoolers and fully stocked luxury hotel rooms paid for by their parents.

My parents and I are staying five minutes away in a home. After dinner and hanging at one of the "uncool" pools of the desert oasis hotel, aka one of the pools occupied by floaties, not mixed drinks, my parents can't get ahold of my sister. Her phone is off, so it is time to grab the duplicate key to her hotel room and find her.

Upon entering the suite, we find what resembles the set of a raunchy rap video or a rock and roll memoir, whatever suits your story. There are empty bottles of Grey Goose thrown into piles alongside plastic gas-station bottles of vodka. Shattered glass litters the hotel carpet. Both cheap and very expensive bottles of alcohol cover the marble kitchen counter. There are piles of glass on the ground below the balcony, thrown off in an attempt to fool either cops or parents, but to no avail.

In the shower, on the bed, under the bed, everywhere, liquor. A lone pack of Swishers sits on the finished wood table next to the room-service menu.

Kayla's best friend, Tianette, ends up in the ER that night, suffering nearly irreversible brain damage from the sheer amount of alcohol she consumed.

The near miss with T was not the first case I would witness during my time attending Newport Coast High School. Several people would not be as lucky as T had been that night.

In the years after pills were brought to the high school arena. Several kids never woke up.

My friend never woke up.

My mother sends Kayla to therapy following the incident. It doesn't work out well. The therapist suggested Kayla stopped drinking. Kayla, all of fourteen, responded,

"There is no way I will ever stop drinking. I love the way it makes me feel, and you can't do anything about that."

The therapist then refused to work with Kayla. She did, however, ask my mother to bring me in. The therapist felt it necessary because I had been around when the "traumatic" incident occurred.

Dr. Thompson's office is vast. She has a kind face and her eyes wrinkle at the sides when she smiles. As I thoughtfully answer her questions, sinking deeper into the luxurious dark-brown leather sofa, she sporadically purses her lips gently and nods in approval. She has a little metal ball desk ornament that I find interesting. But it is not necessarily calming.

Books line the shelf behind her.

I tell Dr. Thompson everything. I go into great depth because she asked. I unload the burden of feeling that the weight of the world is upon my shoulders and my shoulders alone. I explain my constant preoccupation with feeling that I need to change the world, the feeling that I am not doing enough to help, and as a result, spend most of my time worrying, depressed. On top of that, I feel a tremendous amount of pressure to be the best at everything. I tell her that I feel gray most of the time.

The psychiatrist questions me about things I am afraid of and in the moment, I remember riding the elevator up to her office. The recall brings to my attention that I hesitated to get in the elevator. I confess this. She assures me that I have a phobia of elevators. I leave with a small prescription for Ativan, an anti-anxiety drug, and all is well. The phobia is why the world looks gray; I am afraid of elevators.

And so it begins.

My mother kept the prescription for Ativan. I don't ever remember taking it.

What is interesting about Dr. Thompson's forced diagnosis and coinciding prescription for Ativan is that Ativan is linked to worsening depression in people already suffering symptoms of depression. The risk of increased suicidality is highest among children and young adults, and Ativan is not even proven adequately effective for anything in children under 12. While Dr. Thompson is diagnosing a pseudo phobia as a source of my angst, she simultaneously prescribes a medication that can lead to suicide, *especially* at the young age of eleven. (See Appendix A.)

Dr. Thompson M.D. (psychiatrist): May 2003
Medications: Synthroid
Reason for Visit: sibling trauma (sister)
A/P: Rx Ativan

Locker Assignments, New Friends, and Queenie

Newport Coast Middle School is within the larger Newport Coast High School or "Coast." I begin middle school, seventh grade, at the same time my older brother, Isaak, is going into Senior Year. Because of its vast age range, the school is by default, intimidating to enter as a seventh grader. My sister had attended a different middle school, one for the Arts, but is now also beginning Coast as a freshman.

For most, the first weeks of seventh grade are spent clinging to the social structures of the elementary school that funneled into Coast. But I had already become friends with the Jefferson girls.

Holly, Emma (a friend of mine from Coastal View) and I, along with a few other Jefferson Elementary girls, spent the last week of summer preparing collages for the insides of our lockers. We purchased locker shelves, magnetic pen holders, and mirrors, and we're excited to set them all up.

Holly is the same girl I used to race at swim meets. In the weeks before the start of classes, I'd branched out as far as one other school; Jefferson. I'd become close friends with Holly: my number-one competition in swimming.

After a run in at the local market, and a subsequent chat about their daughters, Holly's mother called mine to get us together. Holly was having trouble with a few mean girls because to her athletic talents. She excelled in almost every sport she tried. Realizing the similarity, they set up a time for us to go swimming and the rest is history. Holly and I became friends almost instantly and inseparable shortly after that. It was exciting to have a friend from Jefferson. And it was interesting that it was Holly. Kali versus Holly had always been the swim coach's focus.

The blind assignment of our lockers is disheartening. It shakes things up. Holly and my Coastal View Elementary friends could not be situated any farther from me. I am assigned a locker in the middle of what seems like an entire school of people from Westbluff. I did not know one person from Westbluff. Although their school is only ten minutes from my home, it feels like an alien community. Jefferson Elementary, situated within the Yacht Streets, is much more familiar.

The girls I have lockers next to are from a whole different world, one that has an obvious Queen and she seems to be much different than me. She is from the last of the five public elementary schools that funnel into Coast. Her name is Tessa.

Protected

As a measly seventh-grader, running into Isaak and his friends made my day. His friends would chant my name. Isaak would swing me over his shoulders and fake yell at younger guys walking by that he would "kill 'em." It was like Christmas morning to be acknowledged by Isaak on campus, or anywhere really.

Isaak and his friends rule the school. And Isaak, specifically, is King of the pack.
See below:
A) Varsity baseball player
B) Homecoming King
C) Very smart but too cool to pay attention to overly strict teachers (which led to legendary events like the time he convinced his entire class to stand on top of the desks in protest of their teachers' bad attitude.)

To carry on the legacy, I organized the same event five years later, after being placed in the same teacher's fourth-period social studies class.

I am protected in the most literal sense. At one of our school's football games, I watched Isaak knock some kid out for making a rude comment about me.

One lucky Tuesday, as we are lining up in rows for attendance, wearing our very unattractive PE outfits, Maddox, a football player and close friend of Isaak, walks over from the science building.

"Hello, Maddox!" Mr. Schuyler shouts in his baritone voice. As Maddox approaches, Coach Schuyler clears his throat, "This is one of my favorite players of all time, kids. Listen to what Maddox tells you." He throws his arm around Maddox's shoulder.

"Why thank you, Coach," Maddox replies.

And then, I catch his eye. And, in front of all three PE classes sitting on the pavement that afternoon, Maddox shouts out to me:

"Yo! What's up, 'Lil Wheel! Aw man! You got the Little Wheel, Coach Schuyler. She's the best. Hey, Kali!"

Grinning like a dork, I respond, "Hi Maddox!"

"I've got to get to class, just thought I would say hello," Maddox continues.

"Always good to see that beautiful face of yours. Get your fine ass to class, Boy!" Mr. Schuyler shouts.

"Have a good one, Kali. See you tonight. I'm coming over after practice," Maddox says before turning around.

Although my olive skin isn't prone to blushing, my face is hot. I am on top of the world. Maddox strolls back toward the science building.

"You're Isaak Wheeler's little sister?" Mr. Schuyler asks in a more delicate way than usual.

"Yes!"

"Great guy, great guy. I love Isaak. Tell him to play for me, would ya?" Mr. Schuyler adds.

"Yeah!"

"Good," Mr. Schuyler says. He turns to face the center of the class. "Now, for the rest of you scoundrels. I've got three words: Be. On. Time. BE ON TIME!"

Walking the Mile

Tessa and her group of girls from Westbluff and me and the girls from Coastal View all have PE class together. Eventually, our groups begin to meld with each other.

Every Friday we run the mile. And every Friday, I try to outrun my prior week's record. I am hoping to report a six-minute mile to my triathlete father.

Tessa and her friends, without a second thought, walk the mile: paying no mind to Mr. Schuyler standing in the middle of the track with a clipboard. His multicolored Ray-Ban sunglasses reveal their spectrum under the Southern California sun. "Let's get it going, girlies!" he would shout, hoping to speed up their leisurely walking pace. It is impossible not to love this six-foot-six, barrel-chested coach.

For Tessa and her crew, the Friday mile is a moving assembly of girl-talk. They are always laughing, playing with the boys who don't have anyone to talk to and tying up their PE shirts as crop tops, rolling the legs of their blue NCHS-emblazoned shorts five times, rather than the moderate three.

The day I chose to walk the mile was the day that my transformation into rebellious high schooler began. My drive to impress authority figures softened as I began to enjoy myself.

"Oh my gosh, I'm so sorry for being late," Tessa says, bounding into our seventh-grade science class, overly exuberant and audibly apologetic. She knows the teacher will forgive her. It is the same routine every day. She remains standing as she flicks her hair over her shoulder, smacks her gum and then turns around to shush the kids behind her who think it's funny, making the sincere effort to keep the teacher from looking foolish.

Every day she wears a different, brightly colored Victoria Secret thong above her Abercrombie and Fitch denim skirt. Her thongs are part of her outfit, along with something from Abercrombie and Fitch and her hair straightened and bobby-pinned away from her face or up in a ponytail wrapped carefully with a feminine bow.

What is fascinating about Tessa is her ability to befriend everyone. Tessa is kind to every person she meets. She may have been overly friendly to a few teachers and older boys, but bottom-line; it was awesome. She is inclusive and exclusive at the same time. She is an anomaly to me. The boys love her, but she doesn't sleep around. She has a boyfriend: Liam. I have never met anyone who knows as many people as Tessa did. Her superlative in eighth grade, fittingly, was "Social Butterfly." (I got "Best Smile" and ironically took the worst photograph of my life. I convinced myself that the yearbook girl was playing an evil joke on me when I found the one photograph I begged her not to print--we are upside down and I am all gums and squinty eyes--printed in the yearbook.)

Tessa accepts everyone and teaches the rest of the kids to do the same. She is refreshing in a world of drone-like safety. The only people who don't like Tessa were those who haven't met her. This statement is especially true when it comes to parents.

Tessa and I are opposites from an outsider's perspective; our upbringing, behavior, and academic approach: everything. Nevertheless, between the two of us, we have the resources to master any type of situation. Tessa quickly becomes my number one, go-to girl.

The barrier between Tessa and me is shattered one day when I ask her best friend and lab partner, Kendall, for a pencil. I look around helplessly for someone else to ask, but they are all fixated on their labs.

Kendall is always with Tessa. Like vanilla and chocolate, they match in some way, every day. They even talk the same. Kendall, however, has a softer voice. She is quiet, and her blue eyes speak volumes.

Tessa is the person who beams a huge smile and introduces herself, while Kendall will eventually introduce herself and then push her hands into the farthest depths of her back pockets. Kendall reserves showing her generosity, outwardly, for a special few. Kendall has wispy, blonde hair, as opposed to Tessa's thick brown hair, but they wear it the same length as well as up in a ponytail on the same days as one another, with the same type of bow.

My initial question is answered with a kind, "Oh! Sure!" and a simultaneous digging into a well-organized shoulder bag, pulling out the Victoria Secret pencil case I wanted so badly. Kendall hands me one of her pastel-colored mechanical pencils which is rebellious, in a careless way, as mechanical pencils are forbidden because the Scantron reader can't read their lead.

At that moment, I knew we'd be friends.

It was Kendall who invited me over to hang out with their big group of churchgoers who trek across the football field to Kendall's house on Tuesdays to get ready before "Small Groups" that night at the church.

A Good Kid

In January of eighth grade, I get my annual physical from my general practitioner, Dr. Jane. She shares her office with her son, another general practitioner, Dr. Scott. I see whichever doctor is available. Dr. Jane notes only good things on my medical chart. I am not on any medications other than my usual, Synthroid, and I am thriving.

Dr. Jane M.D. (GP): January 26, 2005
Medication: Synthroid for Hashimoto's
Reason for Visit: sports physical
Comments: "straight-A's," NCHS since 7th grade, skis, swims, Jr. Lifeguard, dance

One Girl's Strength

Tessa is the type of girl whose strength I can't even fathom. She couldn't have grown up in a more different fashion that I had, but my parents quickly became hers. Tessa became my mother when my mother couldn't reach me. She can navigate her tangled world as well as run everyone else's around her.

Tessa plays a huge part in not allowing me to carry out things when I was messed up. She read my mind and was in the right place at the right time, multiple times. Tessa shows up in my bedroom at my parents' house, unannounced, because "she had a feeling," or because I didn't answer texts after a distressing phone call with her.

She comes all the way from her grandparents' home on the Island to make me laugh. This Island has only one entrance point via land so it can get traffic-y, depending upon the day. It was a whole different community down there. A lot of people rent beach houses along the boardwalk that encase the island, but the bridge over is also the quickest route to the bigger beaches, i.e. The Wedge, a renowned surf spot. Tessa's street, Coral, is only a few streets away from where the twenty-five cent ferry picks up passengers to cross the bay to the peninsula.

Tessa never talked about her past. When she did, she disguised it beneath the self-deprecating humor. If asked about her parents, she'd say something like, "they're a joke," or "I don't even care." She kept quiet regarding any emotion surrounding her situation. She loved her grandparents and their little home on the Island. And our entire group of friends loved her grandparents too. They were "Grandma" and "Grandpa" to us. I never knew their actual names.

I'll always link Tessa to the nights that she unintentionally saved me from my situation, my boyfriend or myself. A wave of new-car smell mixed with Bvlgari cologne emanates from the blacked-out window as it rolls down to reveal Tessa in the front seat beside Elijah. The signature Rolex identifies him as a member of the local gang, the Lords.

The Lords served as our chauffeurs on the weekends. They were always getting into trouble, but they were all rich enough to buy their way out.

"'Sup, Kali?" Elijah says, his hand on the varnished wood of the stick shift.

Tessa would jump out and greet me with a warm hug.

"Are you good?" she would ask, sincerely.

That smell is one I will never forget. It washes over me as the protective shield Tessa was on those nights.

Hanging with Z-Boys:
I Thought I Was Penny Lane

Kendall's older brother, Jayden, is one of a large group of "cool" guys in the grade above us. The sophomores are a rowdy group, and these boys lead the pack. The boys play music and dress like reincarnates of Jimmy Hendrix, Jim Morrison, Robert Plant and Bob Dylan. And Tessa, Kendall and I are their biggest fans. Since us girls are obsessed with the '60s—especially the music side of things on my end—their style works out quite nicely.

I am used to "hippy-izing" my brother. Isaak is the singer of his band, Zed Leppelin, and aside from helping out with some of the high notes at practice, was responsible for his outfit when they performed last year at lunch in the quad. I was proud of Isaak up there, howling into the microphone alongside his band mates, who I had known forever as my other brothers. I spent time distressing my brother's denim and sewing on patches while listening to album after album of sixties rock groups.

The boys are a bad bunch of kids, though. The smart ones are mixed in there, once in a while, but the group of them altogether is not the group sitting next to me in AP Biology class. They are the guys who the school security knows by name and hassles regularly.

At school, Jayden and the gang ignore us. But once we are all over at Jayden and Kendall's, we have the time of our lives together.

A couple of the guys are more elusive than the rest. Jaxx Moreau, an avid partier, and well-known womanizer will just go missing. I feel like he doesn't have to follow the same rules as the rest of us. I am not even sure he goes to school full time. He comes to school, but most of the time I see him driving away or heading toward the parking lot, no backpack, no school supplies, just a mechanical pencil in the back of his jeans and maybe, a book. I subconsciously reason that Jaxx had some special exception to do anything he wants to do at any time. I think he might attend a different school part-time. He acts like, dresses like and looks like he is already in his twenties. He is a mystery to me; it's enticing. And, he is, by far, the cutest one. When all the other boys went right, Jaxx went left and said, "Fuck right" while he turned the opposite direction.

Kendall's mom, Mrs. Bay, is the most involved, and honestly the most fun mom I have ever met. She will drive us to wherever, whenever. On a Wednesday, Mrs. Bay took the four boys—Jaxx, Jayden, Liam and Tanner--and us three girls all the way up to Venice Beach. It was the middle of the school week! But, the boys had seen Dog Town and Z-Boys, learned to skate on dolphin boards, and had to grind the empty pools and ride their dolphin boards down the long ramp to the beach that they had seen in the film.

Kendall, Tessa and I made up the film crew for their skate film. We worked until dusk on catching them in the perfect light. They fly up the sides of the pool, grind atop the rim, swivel their boards and race back down. It's a beautifully choreographed dance the way they just miss the next skater coming back up from the other side of the pool, seeming to complete the geometric design of their route. They were weaving themselves a flower of life in their repetition. I don't think I'll ever forget the orange sky over the water, the sun speckling the sand in shallow shadows only touching the places that were close enough to its rays before casting a gray shadow over half the beach and then the entire beach, within minutes.

We love Mrs. Bay. I particularly appreciate the snacks she provides us every afternoon; ranging from buttered, grilled tortillas to tacos and casseroles. And, there is always Ovaltine! The first day, after hanging at Kendall's, I quickly divulge the name of my new favorite drink to my mother, thinking she will be interested and buy it. Se laughs at me instead.

I guess it isn't a new thing.

Kendall and Jayden's house is across the street from Coast. Due to its proximity and our hormone levels, it tends to serve as the local hideaway and hookup center for the high school.

Mrs. Bay prides herself on the fact that the "cool" kids go to Kendall and Jayden's.

She also likes her title of "Snowplough Mom" that the local newspaper had deemed her: proving my mother's point exactly, that Mrs. Bay was strange. But I could care less. Her story spread across multiple pages of the paper with a full-size photograph of her and her best friend, another "Snowplough Mom."

"See!" my mom shouts, holding up the newspaper, "I told you, it's not normal to be so involved, Kali. It's odd."

"So what?" I say, not buying into the drama in my doorway.

"So, it's weird! It's weird to just take my daughter to Los Angeles without telling me in the middle of the week!"

"You're still thinking about Venice?" I say.

"Yes! Yes, I am. Because you can't just kidnap my child..." my mom's face softens as she realizes I'm laughing at her being so ridiculous and breaks into laughter too, "It's weird, hang out with me, I am cool!"

I had to talk my mom into approving my new group of friends, and their mother. She was not thrilled, which was funny because I had to beg my mom to let me go to church.

The One Provision

Kendall's dad is a pastor, but I have never see him at Lighthouse: the mega church in our community, actually referred to as Lighthouse Village now because of its immensity. Lighthouse Church is where the girls go every Tuesday evening after walking home together in a pack. Specifically, Lighthouse's Junior High Ministry, a campus specifically the middle-school that offers live music, food, games, and all the middle-school students in the county. Newport Coast is not the only school that parties at the church for Tuesday evening Small Groups. The few other middle schools in the area show up too. It is the best.

"Small groups" is a program within the middle school section of Lighthouse Church. Every Tuesday evening, every middle schooler in the city is invited to hang out at the church, sing along with a band heavily influenced by current alternative pop music and meet in groups of a dozen for a half hour before listening to more music and eating more snacks with everybody else your age in the county (it felt like).

All of the buildings within Lighthouse Church are beautiful, state of the art. But, the junior high facilities are next-level. Attending a service within Lighthouse Church's Junior High is like going to a Switchfoot concert, except the people are all the same age and there is more space to roam.

The Junior High Campus is completely separate from the main campus within Lighthouse Church and the vibes are always rocker-chic. Mood lighting perpetually on fleek, low-key disco balls hanging from the forty-foot ceiling, not to mention, hot chocolate, several loveseats, pool tables, anything you want, they've got it in surplus at Lighthouse.

Junior High Ministry at Lighthouse is the place to be on Tuesday evening. After the dance party, the lights come up a little and all twenty or more groups break off and meet in a designated area within the church grounds. For instance, we met on level four of the third building. It was the office of the church's Director of Art.

Groups are composed of about nine friends and led by a twenty-something volunteer. Girls go with girls, guys with guys, there is no gender mixing for the twenty minutes held for small group discussion. We discuss life, any issues that come up and sometimes a theme. We clown around for a good amount of time, say a prayer, and head back to the main campus to listen to more music, say another prayer and close out.

No one liked leaving that place.

If you are new, you can ask to join whatever small group you want. But, there is a voting process. If the group has room for a new member and if they all agree they want you in their group, you are accepted.

To hang out with Kendall and the squad, and be driven around by Mrs. Bay you have to go to church. So, in exchange for the free designated driver and house to crash in, everyone went to Small Groups and sometimes Sunday service too.

Mrs. Bay did everything for us, spent all her time with us and spent all her money on us; but, the one thing that was not debatable was going to church. And it was a hard and fast rule. You better believe you would not be allowed at the house the next week if you bailed on church. I saw the reaction. "No way Kendall! They didn't come to church and they promised," she would motion for Kendall to hang up, and when Kendall did not Mrs. Bay would continue: "Sorry! You can't come because you have to come to church with us if you do and you won't, sorry!" she's shouting so that the person on the other line can hear through the phone's speaker.

Mrs. Bay prides herself on the van full of teenagers, sober or not, that she hauls to church on Tuesdays and Sundays. She does not condone drinking. However, she is our designated driver every weekend. She says she would rather have us in a car with her, drunk, than behind the wheel, drunk. Her logic makes sense.

Abiding by the "church" rule allows us to do everything else. Anybody that Kendall or Jayden invites can come over on Tuesdays. Only a few of us can do stuff like trade clothing. Kendall has an enormous closet full of the trendiest clothing, vintage fur coats and boots; everything. Tessa and I are the only ones who can swap with her.

And also, only the three of us, plus Jayden's closest friends—Liam, Jaxx, Tanner—can spend the night. We can all sleep in the living room together as long as we have separate blankets.

"It will make you drunk. Take it," Tessa says. She hands me a white pill. She throws two round, battery-size pills into her mouth. "I'm serious. It will make you drunk without drinking."

"You girls ready to pick up the boys?" Mrs. Bay asks from the driver's seat.

Mrs. Bay looks at us three sardines, Kendall, Tessa and I, in the backseat through the rearview mirror. Her eyes sparkle with her unique blend of charm and curiosity. I swear Mrs. Bay is perpetually jolly. Maybe it's because her husband is a minister.

"Duck down, grab something and take it," Tessa whispers. She nearly pushes me onto the floorboards with a shoulder nudge and then brilliantly responds to Mrs. Bay, "Let's go! I'm starving!"

When I took my first Soma and subsequently my first recreational prescription drug, I did so to feel drunk without getting into trouble. I was immediately fascinated by the new world it opened up. I could pop one odorless pill and feel just as good as I did after drinking seven beers. The best part was that it was parent-proof. There was no trace of having done anything wrong.

It cost Tessa ten dollars to purchase one in 2005. A couple of years later, I get a sandwich bag of two different strengths, fifty of each, completely free. They are garbage by 2007. Once Newport got ahold of the real stuff, Somas were trash.

People used Somas as an "add-on" pill. They were good to throw into the mix to enhance the effect of whatever pill you wanted to take. On the more serious side, these seemingly harmless pills have some devastating consequences, especially combined with other things. (See Appendix B.)

In the back of Mrs. Bay's Suburban, Tessa, Kendall and I wait for the group of drunk guys Mrs. Bay is driving to the next party, in exchange for a promise to go to church with us in the morning.

I hope Jaxx comes.

My friends say I can have any guy in the entire school. I want the one guy who does not care about anyone, let alone my younger, and in comparison, kind of nerdy self. Jaxx is the only guy I want attention from, even if he is drunk or high or whatever Jaxx does. I see something in Jaxx Moreau that others don't. It's hard to explain the feeling when you know that you're seeing someone, unlike other people, see him.

The herd of intoxicated upperclassman shoves each other as they laugh their way toward our car parked in the middle of the Newport Coast Shopping Center.

"Bro, I can't even..." Liam says.

Liam is Tessa's on again, off again, mostly on again, unofficial boyfriend.

Liam chuckles as he takes a swig out of his water bottle, which clearly is not full of water. I say this not because it isn't clear because it is, but because it's Friday night in Newport. He continues in his surfer-type slang that no one outside this three-mile radius would probably understand:

"I'm out. It's gnarly; it's like she...I dunno Bro, it's next level, ya know?"

Tessa swoons in the seat next to me. She leans over and whispers, "I seriously love him, not even kidding," and then leans back and stares me right in the eyes, throwing her hands into the air to drive the point home. "I'm serious. It's too funny." She mumbles into the window of the Suburban, "I fucking love him, Kali. I fucking love that kid," before clasping her palms tightly back together and sealing them neatly between her thighs, re-crossing her legs, careful not to pull a Brittany Spears/Paris Hilton in her denim skirt.

Kendall has her sights on Tanner, who is the third of the three musketeers.

"Are we picking up Tanner, Mom?" Kendall asks.

"No sweetie, not unless he calls. Jayden said he is with Jaxx tonight. Oh!" Mrs. Bay jumps as her old-school Samsung starts ringing. It's one of those piano default tones. "Speaking of the devil..." she says before answering it.

Kendall turns to me, throwing her arms into the air as if mock praying.

"Hello Jaxx, my sweet boy, are you coming to church tomorrow?" Mrs. Bay asks in her usual nun-like voice. Her voice only gets lower when she is talking to the boys trying to coordinate their drunken rides, and they are acting belligerent. "Well, Jaxx, you know the rules…"

Kendall grabs the phone out of her mom's hands. Kendall is sitting in the row of seats in front of Tessa and me in the very back. She tacitly puts the phone on speaker.

Jaxx is hammered.

"Just pick me up please," Jaxx whines, but he sounds adorable all the same. "Please come now, I'm waiting for you. I need you here now. Please, Diane."

God, he's adorable even when he's plastered.

"Come to church Jaxx!" Kendall shouts into the phone.

"Kali? Wait…Hello?" there's a bit of a pause and then, "Are you with Kali Rae?" He suddenly sounds sober.

Kendall and Mrs. Bay both turn around in their seats to look at me and give me that K-I-S-S-I-N-G nursery rhyme look. Mrs. Bay makes sure to leave Jaxx hanging just a second longer than usual, "No, that was Kendall… Why, Jaxx? Did you want to see Kali?" she asks strategically, turning to wink at me in the back seat.

"Wait, who is this?" Jaxx sounds upset like he forgot what he is doing on the phone with a middle-aged woman at 1:00 a.m. on a Saturday.

"Jaxx, this is Mrs. Bay. Where are you? We are coming to get you, and you are coming to church with all of us, including Kali, so find a cross street. We are picking up Liam and Jayden right now."

"Wait…" Jaxx seems to have been interrupted and is yelling away from the speaker "Yeah, for sure. Let's do it, Bro. I'm so down. Hey, what are you doing? Hey!"

Click.

"This may be tough," says Mrs. Bay as she hands the cell phone back to Kendall.

The handle of the Suburban's passenger door repeatedly clanks until Mrs. Bay unlocks the car to let Jayden jump into the passenger seat. The side door of the Suburban violently swings open. Liam, Tanner, a couple of random guys, and two girls pile into the car.

Kendra, a girl in Tanner's grade from my Elementary school, sits on Tanner's lap. Mrs. Bay's classic church-check is waiting in the wings.

"Kendra, are you coming to church with us in the morning?" she continues. "You all can spend the night at our house tonight, BUT you have to come to church in the morning," she says jovially.

"Mom. Shut up," Jayden shouts turning up the volume of the radio. Moments later, he turns it all the way back down to pick up the phone. "Jaxx! We're coming, Bro. Yes, yes! Aha yeah..." And then holding the speaker turning to his mother: "Mom! Turn around and go to the Zianni pool. We've got to grab Jaxx.

The Quintessential Sk8r Boi

Tessa and a group of older guys and I are down at my friend's private beach. It's the same beach my friends used to throw me a surprise party in sixth grade. The secluded spot now serves as the perfect place to drink whatever alcohol we had managed to get together for the weekend ahead.

Tonight is a little bit different than the others because I am supposed to "hook-up" with aka kiss with tongue in Newport lingo, an upperclassman by the name of Derrick. My upperclassmen friends had been trying to get us together for almost a year now. But, only now, with some planning, but not much, on Tessa's part, were we finally together in a place that had some privacy. Tessa made sure Derrick would be coming tonight before we agreed to come hang out with the crew.

Tessa runs up to me as I jump down from the wooden steps onto the beach. It's pitch black outside. The flames from the bomb fire light up the faces of a couple of guys a few yards away. I don't see Derrick.

"He's waiting for you!" Tessa is excited.

"Well, that's awkward…where?" I say. Butterflies are jumping around inside my chest, but I act cool. I'm calm and collected.

Breathe Kali.

"Come on! Who cares? Go make out with Derrick!" Tessa says into the darkness. "He's over there, I promise. Just walk over there, he'll do the rest." Tessa giggles.

It is so dark; I nearly face-plant making my way through the damp sand to where Derrick is waiting. Tessa set everything up. All I have to do is walk over to him.

The sand is cold on my toes, and the waves echo off the cave walls behind us. Mansions line the coast above. The light from their windows doesn't make it to the sand below. They look like jack-o-lanterns from here. It is pitch-black from the moment you step off the wooden stairs and onto the sand.

Derrick is standing away from the group, out of sight in the darkness. He only says a few words before I found out how beer tastes on another person's tongue.

Okay, I did it!

On the way back, Derrick stops me before helping me over the crevice where the sewer water drains into the ocean. He holds his hand out like a classic gentleman in his rolled up denim. I can imagine how sparkly his eyes would look in the sunlight. I grab his hand, and he lifts me over the water.

Derrick is a year older than me. But he is well known within my group of new friends. He lives in the Yacht Street, a neighborhood teaming with Coast students. The Yacht Streets even have a network of parents who have each other on speed-dial to alert one another if they saw a party or noticed a new car parked on their street. The Yacht Streets is the neighborhood where secrets are never really secret. Everyone knows everything; it's like putting a magnifying glass on the normally way too involved community of affluent stay at home parents.

This community idea worked to my advantage in the current situation, as Derrick had already been scoped out by several sources. He is the classic surfer-dude from a kind family that has lived in the same house Derrick's entire life, just like me. Even Kayla likes Derrick, which is part of the reason I want to stay with him.

Months later, I find myself face to face with Derrick again. This time, I want to know more. He has grown much taller in the months since the night on the beach; he thinned out to become even more handsome.

Now, the sandy-blonde surfer boy with the megawatt smile is clinically dreamy. And I'm the one he's looking to date.

Swoon.

One afternoon Derrick invites me out to lunch. Walking with him past the security guards, I feel special as a freshman going out to lunch. And then I notice something on his car. His tinted, tricked-out SUV has new plates: DRTYRDN.

My feelings for Derrick are not strong enough to disregard another embarrassing event like those license plates and the way Derrick's tried to deny that he had anything to do with them. I think those license plates were the beginning of that relationship's decline.

Serious stuff, huh?

Things were so serious between Derrick and I, that we would do things like; hang out of his bedroom window to do keg stands with the leftover keg he moved under his windowsill from his brother's party the night before.

It was probably a few events, plus the initiation of those license plates, that caused the first hemorrhage in the relationship. It was my ability to get annihilated drunk that caused the next. one.

Part II:
Freshman Year

Aruba: Setting Goals

Every year we take a family vacation. And this year it was my turn to bring a friend. My brother won't be traveling with us. He is busy at school. I decide to bring Tessa. As soon as we get to the hotel, Tessa and I throw down our luggage; change into bikinis and head for the pool. There are a few pools and even a lazy river; we are in paradise.

Looking down at my almost flat stomach, I pinch the little pooch above my metallic-silver, string bikini bottoms.

"Oh god," Tessa says, catching me in the act. She rolls her eyes, flawless body and all.

Tessa is five-foot-five, one-twenty and looks like a swimsuit model in a bikini.

However, I began to understand Tessa better when, one afternoon, Kendall told me that Tessa had undergone a major transformation between sixth and seventh grades.

Tessa, I guess, had lost more than sixty pounds in just the three months of summer vacation, and had transformed herself from the "fat" girl (her word not mine) into the most popular girl at her school, just in time to assimilate into the middle's school/high school population.

"I need to lose ten pounds," I say. I can read Tessa's annoyance, so I add, "I would be happier."

As I say this to Tessa, I find that I am deciding to commit wholeheartedly to lose those ten pounds this time around. Saying it out loud makes it a dare rather than an idea. Now I am putting myself up to it.

"You're a joke. Kali, please don't be dumb," Tessa responds.

Splashing through the light-blue water, Tessa kicks away from me and climbs onto a light pink inner tube. She grabs one for me too. I feel my shoulders burn in the Aruban sun. I can tell we are closer to the Equator.

"I mean, I'll do it with you, but like whatever," Tessa adds.

I bounce off the pool floor until I am sprawled on top of the water, moving slowly down the lazy river. I grab the inner tube but ditch it moments later. I like the idea that without any help, a body can keep itself above water.

I tip my chin and see that annoying pooch right above my bikini bottoms.

I would be so much more desirable. I'd do anything. And then that voice kicks in.

Prove it, Kali.

Dares are my specialty. And I was about to show the world how tough I was; there was nothing that could stop me from being whatever I wanted, and I wanted to lose at least ten pounds.

That night in the hotel room that attached to my sister's suite, I have an idea.

"Let's go out!" I say.

"Yeah, okay Kali," Tessa says. She turns to me, "Will your parents even let us?"

My parents were very strict with the rules because there had been a kidnapping on the island a few years back. It was an American college student. We are not allowed to go out alone when the sun goes down. Not even if Kayla comes with us.

"I'm not going," Kayla mumbles from the other room in the suit.

"Got it. Thanks, Kay," I say and look to Tessa. "Why is she such a bitch?"

"Um, she's not," Tessa says, "Relax." She laughs.

"I can just ask. We could stay within the Marriott area and be back before dark. Let's find a drink,"

"Yeah, oh-kay," Tessa says, rolling her eyes characteristically.

She doesn't mean it. I can tell she's just enjoying having a family.

Tessa didn't grow up with parents. She lived with her wonderful grandmother and grandfather in a little duplex apartment. I never saw the way the differences affected us really until that trip to Aruba. I hadn't recognized how blessed I was even to go on vacation. I was thankful, yes, but the fact us siblings would argue because one of us didn't get to bring a friend was ridiculous to me now. I was beginning to see this.

We did end up going out, as well as running back to the Marriott entrance in terror; sand shoveling up behind our roadrunner feet. A group of local boys started following us, catcalling and running up beside us while we walked. We were all a bit on edge about the kidnapping and the beach looked eerily similar to the news reports about it.

A few years later that we learned that the beach we were running from was the beach from the news reports.

I knew it.

I think back to the feeling I had while deep-sea snorkeling around a sunken ship.

In a moment, I went from excitedly exploring the ship to feeling my heart racing and fully utilizing the fins I had rented, in a full-out sprint back to the ladder hanging off the back of the yacht.

"What if that girl is in there?" I shout, panicked, to my father.

He laughs from afar. "Relax! What girl, Kali?"

Our Town's Tony Robbins

Dr. Gary Whittman was the talk of the town. Well not really, but everyone seemed to go to him. He was the town psychologist. He even did a presentation at one of our school's rallies. I stayed quiet the whole time so as not to tell my entire grade that I, indeed, went to him for counseling.

Not long after I start seeing Dr. Whittman, spilling everything I am into the void that I thought was his office, he suggests that I see his friend who is a psychiatrist. Her name is Dr. Jensen. I was only to go to her to see if there was something she could do to help alongside the work I was doing with Whittman every Thursday. The amount of over-sharing I was doing with him, coupled with the intensity of the emotions I feel in general, just as a person, would be cause anyone to be sent me to a psychiatrist.

I wasn't necessarily depressed. No one would have thought anything other than "totally fine" when interacting with me on a social level, but I did have a lot of philosophical questions to mull over. And I didn't have anyone I could talk to that understood where I was coming from on that level.

I don't think anything of Dr. Whittman's referral over to the psychiatrist. I did realize that seeing a psychiatrist was more "heavy-duty" than the very casual appointments with Dr. Whittman.

It wasn't long after seeing Dr. Whittman that I realize all of the specific stories with the specific people attached to them, are probably Dr. Whittman's patients too. The drama that I thought was so unique to me and my secret life played out in his appointments with those particular individuals later in the week.

However, I don't filter myself even after finding out one of the guys I'd been going on about saw Dr. Whittman too.

The prescription of Prozac that followed the single appointment with Dr. Jensen seemed as casual as the entire process. So, the adherence to what this new psychiatrist was instructing me to do to feel even better was a no-brainer.

Dr. Jensen M.D. (psychiatrist): June 16, 2006
Reason for Visit: referral from Dr. Whittman
Medications: Synthroid
A/P: Rx Prozac. Begin at 5mg. Increase by 5mg/week for 6 weeks

A Summer Affair: Gnarls Barkley

After a night of drinking at one of our guy friend's houses, Tessa and I and a group of our friends make it to the Orange County Fairgrounds. There is a concert tonight. It is a group who we'd heard on the radio all summer long. I don't know the band, but I am excited to drink and assemble somewhere.

Almost as quickly as our group arrives, we run into Jaxx and a few other Z-Boys. I follow lead as the group hops over the seat backs to socialize with their boys before the concert starts. It is still light outside. I scan the stadium for people I know, hanging around the outside of the row, hoping to find alcohol and savoring the haze coming over me. (See Appendix D.)

Kendall and Tessa know this crew of boys better than me. Tessa jumps over the seat next to Jaxx who is a few seats down from her boyfriend, Liam, and gives Jaxx a hug. I follow her, but don't know Jaxx well enough for a hug. I don't think he knows how I am.

"Kali, stop!" Jaxx says to Tessa, who is reaching for his drink.

This isn't good.

"Oh, my god. Wait, what?" Tessa says.

It's like the rest of the concert mutes as I realize what may have just gone down.

Did I hear that correctly? Did Jaxx Moreau just say my name—but to Tessa?

Tessa turns her body to face Jaxx directly.

"TES-SA, TES-SA. Are you serious right now Jaxx?" she says.

"Sorry Dude, I'm drunk," Jaxx laughs. He's apparently shocked he said it too.

"Whatever. Do you even know Kali?" Tessa then turns to me and looks back at him. "This is a joke right?"

Well, this escalated quickly.

"Yo, calm down. I know your name," Jaxx says.

"Of course, you know my fucking name. Are we being serious right now?" Tessa says.

"You need to calm down. Relax," Jaxx says.

"You need to relax," Tessa says and grabs for his drink again.

"The fuck out of here," Jaxx says, moving his hand holding the drink further out of Tessa's reach.

This is really bad.

"Seriously? Fuck you Jaxx. Do whatever you want. I don't fucking care," Tessa says.

Whoa, what just happened?

"Whoa, what just happened," Jaxx says, laughing a bit at Tessa's fit.

Tessa pushes past the guys standing in front their seats to get back over to me.

"Kali, Jaxx is off limits," she says.

She seems mad at me for something. What did I do?

"Like I've known Jaxx forever. No matter what, Jaxx is mine, Kali. Like it's always been us. You don't get it. He's off limits," Tessa says.

Tessa is very upset. Not a usual upset. Tessa reacts as if her actual boyfriend, Liam, cheated on her.

She climbs over the seatback of the plastic, stadium chairs and stomps away. Her boots smack the concrete of the outdoor auditorium as she marches all the way over to the section where Derrick is drinking with his friends.

"What's up, babe?" Tessa squeals to Derrick who is visibly drunk.

I watch her chug a drink out of the Orange County Fair plastic, way-too-tall, and way-too-neon-glass.

The boys hoot and holler, egging her on. She swings her arm around Derrick and Brooks. "I love you guys!" she says.

Jaxx and Derrick are in the same grade, but Jaxx is on the fringe of Derrick's group and vice versa. Derrick is a "Yacht-Streeter." Jaxx is, well, a gorgeous, bad ass, bad boy. He spends his weekends with his cousin in Los Angeles who is currently shooting for his hit television show. Jaxx is unreachable to the highest degree.

Tessa's exit coincidentally leaves me right next to Jaxx, and we are both confused.

My best friend just left me to drink with my boyfriend, and her boyfriend is a couple of seats down from Jaxx.

I had never hung out with Jaxx outside of a group of over a dozen. Nonetheless, I had a huge crush on him.

Did he even go to our school? Did he even go to school anymore?

I guess he does know my name...

"Tessa is pissed," he says nudging me with his obnoxiously long drink cup. It was one of those bright pink, bong-looking slushy drinks that, by the smell of it, was not the recipe the fair had served up that night.

"Try some. I made it." He mouths, "For you." He smiles, making it very hard for me to hold it together.

"What's in it?" I yell over the music.

"Vodka...Red Bull," he shouts and then leans in to speak directly into my ear (Where does he learn this kind of a trick?) "And whatever else they put in the drinks here. Where's your boyfriend?"

He puts an emphasis on 'boyfriend,' like my older brother Isaak does before teasing me in front of his group of senior boys (all of whom I had a crush on).

"I dunno," I say, grabbing the drink from his hands and taking a long sip.

"Whoa there. Relax. We've got time."

I just want to stand next to him the rest of the night. He's calming to me.

But, nope, must self-sabotage.

"Tessa is going to kill me, " I say.

He's wearing a black long-sleeve, V-neck, waffle tee and True Religion Jeans. His Jack Purcells are bright white, and his Tiffany's dog tag lies perfectly on his chest. And his leather bracelet, he's perfect.

Everything about him is irresistible to me. And when I hug him, my chin hits right in the middle of his chest. I can wrap my arms all the way around him. Of course, I wouldn't know this yet, since it is still Sophomore Year. I am dating Derrick, who I just got a text about:

Tessa: Derrick is crying. We are leaving. Do whatever. Love You. Xo <3.

I show Jaxx. "Advice?" I ask, eager for his input.

"Nah."

"Anything?"

"Nope. No advice from me. I've got nothing to do with whatever that is," Jaxx says.

He turns back to face the stage and chugs the rest of his drink. He keeps his eyes forward.

"Fuck them. Stay with me," he says and takes another sip of his drink.

He looks over at me with the perfect smirk on his face, says nothing, and turns back around, pulling a silver pack of Newports out of his back pocket. Without looking my way again, he artfully smacks the top of the pack on his other palm.

He is dreamy; tall and his hair has this wave about it. He turns the pack slightly and smacks it a couple more times. His silhouette stays completely parallel to me, stoic as if I'm not there at all. And I love it.

He carefully pulls the red tag, unraveling the plastic harnessing the pack. He fingers a cigarette out and places it at his lips, pulling a lighter out of the inner pocket of his black coat.

"So...what's up?"

Shit. Okay. Leave now, Kali.

I'd lost myself gazing at him and the intensity with which he was ignoring me. Managing some sort of a smirk, I pull the center of my denim skirt down as I very awkwardly crawl over the plastic stadium seat and bolt.

This is the first time I wander off at one of the Orange County Fairgrounds concerts.

My memory is completely disjointed; disconnected. I don't know where I am or why I am there or how I got there. I am not sure when I left Jaxx's side, but I am hoping it was before I got this drunk.

I am riding a security golf cart toward the darkness of the Orange County Fairgrounds parking lot after dark.

I blackout. (See Appendix C.)

A good time later, I arrive at a bright yellow security tent. It's huge, parachute-like inside. It's late. The paramedics have deserted their medical room.

It's just the young driver of the security golf cart, the older man sitting, legs spread, arms crossed (classic power position) and me. The older guy straightens up when he sees me.

"So I hear you're lost," he says.

"Yeah, but I'm really far from everyone now. Where am I?"

"You're safe." He chuckles, "Trust me. You don't seem very trusting...relax. I'll take you back to your friends in a bit."

He questions me about drinking and I answer honestly. His reactions are confusing to me. It's almost as if he is pretending to have authority over me by asking me these questions in his Orange County Fair security windbreaker, but over time, it seems like more of a sick game that these two are playing with me. They find each one of my answers funny. They are almost taunting me.

"You're cute," the older guy says. "Why are you alone here? It's not safe for you to wander around."

He looks me up and down, which in spite of in my drunkenness makes me uncomfortable because my denim skirt doesn't fall right, even with my legs crossed tightly.

"Good thing Rogelio found you," the older guy says.

Rogelio is standing in the doorway, leaning against one side, arms crossed.

"And you're 21?" the older man asks.

"Um, yeah," I lie.

"You at least 18?"

"Yes," I lie again.

"Don't be nervous, pretty girl," Rogelio says from the doorway.

"Thank you. Please take me back," I say, scared.

They laugh in unison. I black out.

Some time later, I wake up drinking out of an Orange County Fair cup. I am still in the yellow tent. Rogelio is gone. A rush of terror washes over me. I'm alone with the security guard in a tent, who knows how far from the concert. I can't hear anyone outside. It's deserted.

Where is Jaxx?

"Please take me back now. My boyfriend is waiting for me," I plead, "He's mad that I bailed on him. He'll find me! Please."

Somehow I make it back to the entrance of the concert venue. I thank the security guard too many times to disguise my distrust and utter relief that I'd made it back in one piece. I pull my stiff denim skirt down so as not to pull a Britney Spears as I hop off the cart.

"Call me, Beautiful. I've gotchu," the older security man says from his cart.

I don't look back as I run back into the venue. My mind is blown. I hear the band's hit song echo within the cement walls of the outdoor stadium as I sprint back into the concert venue. I'm obsessively looking up at the upper level to find Derrick and then down at the level across the walkway hoping to find Jaxx where I'd seen him before; somebody, I just wanted somebody who was safe to hide beside.

"Derrick!"

He holds a large beer as he leans over the railing to the lower levels. He's drunk, and he captures me with one arm, pulls me into him, and motions for me to open my mouth and tilt my head back. He pours beer down my throat. And, just then, I feel taken care of; the beer is thirst quenching. I am safe.

"You like that, babe? Where were you?"

"The security guar—"

"Brooks!" Derrick shouts.

He almost smacks me in the face as he flags down his inebriated friend. Moments later, I am thrown into the metal bars that separate the next level of seating as Derrick gets a drunken body-slam from Brooks.

I turn around, and Brooks mumbles nonsense to me. Derrick shakes him and completely disregards the fact that he's poured beer all over me.

Derrick turns back around holding his beer even higher in the air and belts out the first line of the chorus. He looks at me like a total fool: eyes red, and a gaze unable to focus.

Gross. Where's Jaxx?

I turn to lean into Derrick and simultaneously scan the crowd while resting on his soft black, Hurley skater hoodie. His jacket smells good: cigarettes, alcohol, and cologne; it reminds me of the night at the barbecue. I look back up at him. I see Derrick for the first time tonight.

Jaxx!

He is walking out of the venue with Liam, laughing obnoxiously. His gaze meets mine as I'm nestled into Derrick's chest.

Derrick is still screaming the lyrics. His words become random sounds, and then he gets really loud with Brooks together now at the chorus. My gaze meets Jaxx's as he looks at me but manages to make sure I feel unseen. He laughs and yells up to the seats above, "Tessa, get your sexy ass down here!"

What the heck? She's dating Liam!

"Jaxx!" I shout before I can stop myself.

He doesn't turn around.

"One second," I say to Derrick, who hasn't really seemed to notice me for the past three hours. I duck under his arm to run after Jaxx.

"Jaxx!" I shout again.

I catch up to him and grab his arm as he's exiting the concert.

"Jaxx!" I'm out of breath.

"Yo, what's up? Where's your boy?" Liam laughs and looks to Jaxx. "Derrick is such a fucking kook, Bro. I'm out."

Disregarding Liam's comments, I stare up at Jaxx but forget everything I was planning to say to him.

"What's up Kali?" he says.

"Oh, well...you just can't go back in if you leave...I didn't know if you knew..."

He takes a gulp from a large cup of beer, "So?"

"So, are you leaving?" I ask.

"Why do you care?" Jaxx says.

"Bro, let's go!" Liam shouts, pacing ahead now.

"I don't," I say.

"Great. Well, it was great seeing you, Kali," Jaxx says and turns away without saying anything more.

He doesn't turn back around either. He just leaves.

I feel a drunken hug from behind.

Guess who is so drunk that he sounds feminine. Derrick lurches into me, and I almost fall to my knees.

"Whoa, whoa! Don't fall, Woman. Don't! You're so drunk, Kali. Look, guys, Kali is so sloppy," he slurs, "Did you fuck Jaxx? Did you fuck the security man?" Unanswered, Derrick continues, "Did you? Hey, hey, Kali. Look at me. Did you? Did you fuck him?"

It was like hearing the buzz of a fan a couple of rooms away.

"Fuck you, Derrick."

I turn to face him, to say something he can hear. There's no use talking to him. He even looks terrible. Derrick stumbles again, sloshing the liquid out of the pink plastic carnival drink-cup. His hoodie is spilled on. And the T-shirt underneath it is awkwardly busting through the top of it: messy and awkward. He looks like a kid.

I throw his arms off of my body. "Get off me, Derrick."

I'm shocked at how easy it is and also how much anger I put into doing so. Derrick grabs me aggressively enough that it takes my breath away. Heat builds inside me.

"What? Oh, you don't like me anymore. Is that it? You don't like being called a slut?" This comment is laughable, in reality, but out of line. At that moment, Derrick becomes irrelevant to me.

"Don't ever touch me again," I say.

"Whoa, Derrick!" A very drunk Brooks steps up against Derrick, allowing me to slip out of the grasp he had re-locked me into.

"He didn't mean it, Kali. He's fucked up. He loves you, like for real. He told me," Brooks says.

"Shut the fuck up, Brooks," Derrick says through squinty eyes.

I readjust my riding skirt and flatten out my impossibly fine hair.

"Thanks, Brooks. But I've gotta go."

I gaze through the strobe lights and stadium seating toward the exit where I'd seen Jaxx last. I hope he's still here. The heels of my Frye boots clank on the cement as I race toward the exit. The yellow shawl I'm wearing feels like a cape as it blows behind me, falling off of my left shoulder. I speed up to meet the rhythm of the song pulsating through the Orange County Fairgrounds.

The fairytale aspect of the night is growing. I notice how perfect the sky is tonight and how blank the slate-colored cement walkway looks reflecting the moonlight, splitting up the two sections of the venue. It is moon-colored and the walkway, turned runway, is wide. I grin as I see Jaxx's smile in my head. I really hope he is still in the parking lot.

The Prozac Experience

Every week after the initial prescription of Prozac, I follow the instructions to up the dosage by 10 mg each week. Around the fourth week, things start getting a bit weird.

In the market, one afternoon, explain to my mother the rainbow aura that comes off of my hand as I wave it, as well as the fact that my world seemed to have finally transformed into color from its black and white state.

In the thick of everything, I decide to do a beach day with my childhood friend Emma. My mother has a call into my general practitioner, Dr. Scott, for the soonest appointment available. I've been having chest pains more and more frequently with each upping of the dosage. My mother has taken issue with my demeanor as well, which I would argue is finally normal. Dr. Scott's office is booked, but I'm told we will be called if there's a way to sneak me in sooner.

I disregard the doctor's appointment that may or may not come and plan a beach day. My mother drops us both off on Opal. After a ferry ride and a few streets, we make it to the sand.

Emma effortlessly steps onto the lava. I have to improvise. With each step I kick my toes under the sand, forming a cool cocoon around each step, the only way to keep from blistering toes. Emma gains body lengths on me walking easily over the boiling sand. She has found a prime spot. I watch as she lays her towel down.

The beach is empty, except for a young family making castles in the sand (thanks Jimi Hendrix).

Emma has been a friend of mine since grade school. She is harsh in an endearing way, now, but as a child, not so much. She was an asshole child. She is the youngest of three and has two older sisters. The middle sister, Emily and my sister were friends growing up. This kind of situation forces a friendship of the younger two. This happened a couple times.

Emma turned out to be a very dependable friend, definitely critical, but loyal. She made a joke on the playground in fourth grade that I'll never forget.

"Kali, you're a pirate's dream!" Emma shouts.

"Huh?" I say, unaware.

"A sunken chest!" she says and laughs so animatedly that it brings the other fourth graders to laugh with her. They look at me apologetically, but they are still laughing.

I knew she meant well, but I'll always remember the joke. Emma was gifted at a young age with the body of a 25-year-old. I, however, was not so lucky. I looked more like a preteen boy up until high school.

Emma was the only friend I had who was also a part of the Gifted and Talented Education (G.A.T.E.) program with me. I was overjoyed to find her in my class the second year. Kids are chosen to attend G.A.T.E. after a test administered alongside the standardized testing. If you score above a certain number, you got to join a class of other kids who scored in the same percentile. For one week, every few months, there were about ten of us, skipped normal school and were relocated to a different school for G.A.T.E.

At G.A.T.E. we not only got a "get out of homework free" card for the entire week, at least of normal school homework, we also got to use our entire brains. We worked to solve complex, tangible puzzles. Our assignments were things like: make this engine work or compose a song or fix the circuit breaker.

It was like a candy store full of the most exciting packages of somewhat intimidating flavors. It was a part of my youth that I will never forget: a breath of fresh air. My grade, for some reason, didn't have many G.A.T.E kids who were also involved in athletics and/or some sort of after-school program, so having Emma there was a treat.

"You're such a nerd!" Emma yells at me.

I give her a thumbs-up and grin like the emoji I use way too often; teeth clenched, mouth like a rectangle. I carefully make my way to her, steps as wide as I can manage, I plunge my toes into the sand, again and again, the sand simultaneously squeaking and thudding with each step.

I unfold my towel. It catches the wind at just the opportune time. The towel straightens itself perfectly as I lay it down. In my mind, a check mark draws itself within a square, and finishes with a cash register "ding!" Perfect. Towel. Laying. Skills.

This had become a skill after so many summer days spent on the beach, from the Junior Lifeguards program in grade school to the now lazy summer days of high school that turned so listlessly into nights on the hot sand of Newport Beach.

I pull the sheer cover-up I had borrowed from my mother over my head and toss it aside. The adrenaline surges through me.

It's game time. Without a word, I sprint toward the water. My heart is beating lightning fast. The sound of my feet hitting the wet sand thumps and then thuds with intensity as I come closer to the water. Sooner than expected, the water smacks up against my shins. A couple slower steps and it hits my thighs.

Not fast enough!

Time to swim.

I bound up over the water, butterfly stroke. A wave breaks up ahead, no fear, I dive, smacking whitewash. Butterfly has always been my favorite stroke. I shocked the competition and their intense soccer moms with my small size. I was usually at least forty pounds smaller and quite a bit shorter than the teenagers I was beating.

The water's temperature feels invigorating against my beating heart. I dive under the oncoming wave; its pressure on my back tumbles and presses me closer to the sea floor and then rips at me, several directions at once. I wait, with almost a sense of vengeance, to kick back to the surface for air. I dig my nails further into the sand. I strengthen my grasp on the seafloor so tight that I can feel the little grains of sand embedding themselves under my nails. I'm almost angry.

Today I feel alive. Why had this feeling been withheld from me for so many years?

I launch myself back to the surface, spring-board-like, and continue swimming, faster and faster. My arms bound out of the water effortlessly. The sound of my hands piercing the water in practiced perfection, sealing my fingers together like a fin, simply adds to the engine I feel propelling me through the surf.

I quickly make it past the break and for the first time, look back to the beach. Emma had followed me in and was making it out of the break zone about now.

"Why are you so far out, Psycho?" Emma spits out the last word almost impressed.

The crash of the wave echoes in the open space of the beautiful June day. I laugh and turn toward the horizon again, kicking a few strokes farther out to mess with her. She follows and soon she is egg-beatering next to me.

"I feel. A-MAZ-ING," I announce to the sky.

Everything is rich in color. I have no fear, none at all. I begin to sing, loudly. What else could I do to release this feeling?

I exhale, "So this is life!"

What starts off as a popular rap song morphs into the same melody sung over by new lyrics consisting of anything and everything that came to mind in the moment: no filter.as it crossed my mind. The sheer volume of my own voice startles me. I am singing loudly, using curse words with no shame. I am free of self-doubt. The newfound power pulses through me. My inner voice is taunting me.

Louder! Louder! Louder! Faster! Faster!

"You think those kids can hear me?" I ask Emma with a hoarse voice.

"Umm, yeah. I'm sure they can, actually."

I feel a little responsible for yelling profanities in my made-up rap song while kids built castles on the beach. There weren't many people on the beach, but the few who were there probably weren't enjoying my song.

"Let's lay out," Emma says and turns to swims back into shore.

"Down," I say, but I linger beyond the surf a bit longer.

Back on the beach, my cell phone is ringing loudly.

I watch Emma fumble through my beach bag to find it. Time to swim in.

Ineffectively wiping my hands on the sandy towel to dry them, I find my phone lodged in the half inch of sand covering the bottom of my messenger bag, colorfully decorated with Mexican patterns, one of three that Tessa, Kendall and I had bought together one Sunday afternoon at the fairgrounds swap-meet.

My soaking-wet hair drips onto the screen, as my sandy fingers wipe the water off and I read the text:

Mom: Dr. Scott can see you today. Meet @ Coral. Can take Emma home after.

Not great planning on my part, but Emma was aware that the text might come and we had decided to come to the beach anyway.

"Ugh! I have to get to the doctor right now. You think we could come back after?"

"Sure, whatever, I'm not really that into staying anyway. It's super hot." Emma towels her face gently and flings herself forward to bring her hair into the perfect messy bun on top of her head. How does she always have perfect hair? I always envied Emma's perfectly textured blonde hair.

"You wanna come with?" I inquire excitedly. "My mom can't drive you home until after, but it's really close and should be short. And also, Let's do something tonight. I need vodka…ASAP. Maybe Elijah can drive us…"

Elijah was a member of The Lords, a rich, local gang.

"Elijah?" Emma says, but also seems fluttery with anticipation. "You sure he would?"

"Of course. They always drive and they always stock the car with Absolut."

Elijah offers alcohol and a safe ride, basically, at any time. However, it is supposed to be for members of their gang, only, plus Alexia and me.

It was wishful thinking to think that Elijah and crew would include Emma. Unless Emma hooked up with one of them (Alexia and I were exempt). Emma was promiscuous and looked a lot older. So, actually, there was a possibility.

"Haha, yeah, sure I'll come. My mom can probably pick me up if I need to get home."

The sand is scalding as Emma stops to slip on her Rainbow sandals. I wince in adrenaline-pumping pain and hop from one foot to the other. It feels good to feel something so intensely. I run the rest of the way to the boardwalk. As we head back towards the ferry, my mom calls. At the same time, a group of men holding red cups call out to us from a balcony on the boardwalk. Emma grabs my bag and reaches in to answer my phone as I am distracted by the prospect of alcohol and new friends.

"Hey, Mrs. Wheeler!" Emma says into the phone.

I gallivant up to the beach house full of thirty-somethings. I turn around to find Emma not happy and not following, instead motioning for me to come back and scowling.

"Yeah, we're almost there...Yeah... No, it's totally fine. Yeah...Yeah..."

Looking puzzled, Emma lifts her hand up next to her head, shaking her head, pissed, in a "What the F are you doing?" expression.

"Kali! Stop!"

I've never heard Emma shaky in her disposition. She is always in control of every situation. The intonation in her voice seems unsure and worried. It is almost exciting to feel that I am shocking her.

A few guys are already coming through the door in their garage holding mixed drinks. The group retreats rather awkwardly, pulling in their extended arms holding drinks, realizing we are definitely not old enough to be hanging out with them, let alone, be served liquor. One of the guys, however, lingers, the red cup drink in one hand and his longneck beer in the other. His Nike sandals give away the fact that he is definitely just renting the place. Actually, the number of backward baseball caps and cut off t-shirts gave that away the moment they yelled at us from their balcony.

"So do you live around here?" one of the out-of-towners asks.

"Yeah, I mean close enough..." I grin and cross my arms over my chest, leaning harder into my left hip. Side note: I'm not blessed in the chest department, so it's better for me to cover up my chest and throw the attention to my legs, or basically anywhere else but my chest.

Emma yanks my arms, flailing them out from the crossed position they were in. I turn to her, a little jerked around, but decide not to argue. I can tell she means business. When Emma means business, you don't challenge her.

We are off.

I awkwardly throw up a peace sign as I turn away, lingering a little too long. I'm a little too interested in a bad situation. The boys who remain on the balcony whistles and I turn around to flash a smile.

"Are you kidding me? Do you want to get raped?" she says to me.

"Whatever. I'm just having fun! YOLO!"

"Yeah, okay," she rolls her eyes. "YOLO doesn't mean get gang-banged on the peninsula, Kali. I told your mom that we were on the way."

Only as I enter the office, on the seventh floor overlooking the yachts parked in the bay do I realize it was a little uncomfortable not to have shoes on. I rub the sand off of the top of my foot with the other foot and it falls on the freshly vacuumed carpet. My mother is visibly upset with my choice of footwear, or lack thereof. Yes, I was barefoot at the doctor's office.

"Kali?"

The nurse's familiar face made me excited.

"Yes!" I jump up, sand falling onto the luxuriously fluffy carpet beneath me. "That's me!"

"You can come with me. Are you coming too, Mom?" she asks, glancing over at my mother as she holds open the door for me.

My mother asks, "You okay out here, Emma?"

Emma looks content and very into her magazine.

"I'm totally fine. My mom is coming."

"Let me just get your vitals," says the nurse when we are in the examining room. She wraps the blood pressure band around my upper arm.

I start giggling. It all seems so serious.

The band tightens and the nurse looks intently at the clipboard she's holding.

The machine beeps and the band loosens.

"Let me just restart this."

She tightens the Velcro and restarts the machine.

The process begins again. It tightens...I start giggling. The machine beeps, the band loosens. I laugh gut-bustingly loud, as the process seems invariably broken to me. But the nurse tries one more time.

I force my mouth closed, but I am still laughing. My sealed lips break inevitably and I laugh out loud, sending the blood pressure machine into its routine. It beeps and loosens.

The nurse is finally laughing with me now. "Okay, we can just try this again in a few minutes."

My mother joins me in the room. She keeps laughing in a sort of worried but amused way. The laugh she would break out in after yelling at my brother.

"Stop playing Superman with your sister! I mean it!"

And my brother would inevitably laugh and ask why she is so upset and she would crumble: breaking her angry expression, melting into a whining, laughing mess; "Isaak...I'm tired of asking you; stop making me laugh."

It was this type of laugh.

I start humming the California Closet Design jingle and bouncing my bare feet on the metal exam table.

"We can triple your closet space! ...Turn your space i..."

My mother thumbs through a magazine, not really looking at it.

Dr. Scott swings through the door.

"Hey you! What's up?" Dr. Scott says.

My mom bursts out laughing. Her eyes get huge as she motions toward me. "This!" she says.

"Hmmm," He looks at her, then over to me.

"What's up with you? I hear your ear hurts and you've been hyper with chest pains."

"I just feel better. You know, like, things are in color; they used to be in black and white. When I swing my hand like this," I swing my hand in front of my face, "I see the rainbow of colors around my arm, like energy or something. I see it. I see everything...like...yeah...finally, I can see."

"I see, I see," he says. "I heard you had fun getting your blood pressure taken."

He manages to say this non-condescendingly, or at least I don't pick up on anything snarky.

"Well, it's just that, I'm obviously fine, but the machine takes so long and then it beeps if you laugh, but it's funny because like I'm obviously not dead, so I don't need to figure out if my heart is beating... You know? My blood is obviously pumping right. Like, it's all so unnecessary and everyone is so serious all the time."

The nurse passes my charts through the door. "She gets it! It was funny!" I say pointing at the nurse.

My mother chimes in: "Her doctor started her on Prozac several weeks back and upped it every week by 5mg for no apparent reason. I don't even know why she is taking it in the first place!"

"Uh huh," the doc shifts from studying my reactions to her comments, back over to my mother's concern. "Dr. Jensen?" he asks.

"Yes. And then, for some reason, she bumped it up to 40mg last week and left for Africa. I can't get a hold of her. Kali has chest pains and she's acting, well, nuts."

"I'm not acting nuts. I just get it now."

"Uh huh," Dr. Scott interjects. "What do you get?"

"Just life...like it sucked. And now it doesn't. But of course, then I must be nuts right? Yep, because that's what my mom says; that's what society says..." I trail off to another thought.

"Look, she's not acting right. She's barefoot, for god's sake, in a doctor's office."

"I get it. I can see you are very...well happy." He searches and then finds the right word looking at me when he says it. Adding, "Although you feel good, I am worried about the chest pain. Let me get what I need to check your ear, and we will figure out what to do with everything else."

He shuts the door, but not completely, behind him.

My mother exhales. "This is truly unbelievable. How do you just leave for Africa?"

I wonder if they clean this floor frequently.

The sand that traveled with me had sprinkled itself sporadically below the exam table. Dr. Scott re-enters and sits down on the swiveling stool in front of the exam table,

"Here's what I got. I am going to consult with a colleague today after you leave, but this is what I know about Prozac. If you have a reaction to an antidepressant like Prozac, it means that it has exacerbated a latent bipolar disorder."

He swivels to the other side of my body, places the cap on the ear-checker device and sticks it into my ear. "So your reaction to this drug didn't cure you of your depression. Instead, it shed light on your bipolar disorder."

"That would make sense!" I shout.

My mother says nothing, but I can read what she is not saying, loud and clear. She wants to argue the diagnosis.

She will NOT take this away from me. I have seen how great things can be. I am not turning back.

This is the answer. This is the answer. He's the doctor. He says so!

He's the doctor!

It's a fact.

I have bipolar disorder...

My inner voice adds a question mark to the last statement. I brush it away.

The simplicity of this diagnosis is astounding to me and also reassuring.

Life was correctly boxed and labeled once more, placed in its correct corner and now equipped with a new label to stick on top.

"I suggest you cut the dose in half immediately. I will update you tonight as soon as I speak with a psychiatrist I know and we will go from there. For the chest pain, let's see if it continues to bother you."

He says all of this while checking my ears, nose and beginning to listen to my heart. He swivels back to the front of me. Confident that he has diagnosed the issue, he stands up, straightens the chart on the cabinet and says he will contact my mother later today.

It all makes sense. This is the reason I feel so different from everyone else. I could use this diagnosis to explain away all of the other things that made me different. All of the other ways I felt I was not the same as the other fourteen-year-olds. This was it! I had found the equation to mate all of my differences. This is an imbalance, something that a pill could balance and fix all of my not-so-desirable (from a categorical standpoint) issues. The reason I felt so different was that I had a disorder. I was bipolar disorder. I mean I was bipolar. I had a category! (See Appendix E.)

Dr. Scott M.D. (GP): August 14 2006
Medications: Synthroid, Prozac
Chief Complaint: earache, chest pains
S: Began Prozac 6 weeks ago at 5 mg, increased to 10mg, 15, 20, 40 mg. Dr. is currently out of town and patient is feeling euphoric.
2 weeks ago: giddiness and less sleep, risky behavior and unable to focus e.g. lit match, placed on tongue and burned tongue.
Chest pain, anxiety, chest pain now, two episodes yesterday
O: laughing, smiling, flight of ideas, positive rational thought and speech not perceived
A/P: Bipolar disorder exacerbated by Prozac. Instructed to taper off Prozac. Message left for psychiatrist and Dr. Hollenberg (psychiatrist), awaiting reply

---

Dr. Scott M.D. (GP): August 14, 2006
Add: Call with Dr. Hollenberg (psychiatrist): taper down to 10-20mg of Prozac. But suggests do not stop to allow patient for review. Also, Ativan should help. However, patient may also use Depakote ER 500mg, if Ativan not effective enough. (See Appendix F.)
Will call patient's mother

Dr. Scott M.D. (GP): August 27, 2006
Add: Patient's mom reports patient went to dance class yesterday behavior is "normal" today too. However, patient has chest spasms, mom wishes to D/C Prozac. Will evaluate for dizziness and chest pain episodes.

Dr. Hollenberg's Advice

Upon discussing with his colleague, Dr. Hollenberg, a local psychiatrist, Dr. Scott decides that I shouldn't discontinue the Prozac, but taper it down. He is advised that Ativan should help and that Depakote ER can also be used if the Depakote is not effective enough.

The medication guide for Ativan warns against using it for a person with depression or psychosis. (See Appendix A.)

My mother expresses her discontent with the idea of me continuing on this new drug, Prozac, and although Dr. Scott has these adverse reactions in his notes, I am not taken off of Prozac. Ten days later, he writes that my mom wishes to discontinue Prozac and also notes the continued instances of chest pain, dizziness and chest spasms.

My behavior ceases to be an issue or at least one that needs immediate medical attention, but my physical health begins to decline.

Part III:
Sophomore Year

The Index Card

Over the prior weeks on Prozac, I had grown to love the feeling of not needing food to sustain my energy levels. I felt lighter when I woke up in the morning, and more energized.

Serotonin Syndrome threw me into a state of euphoria, and I'll do anything to get that feeling back: where all I wanted to do was run around and dive into all the things that I'd push aside in my life up until Prozac illuminated them.

Times were so good that I didn't think twice about the chest pains until it brought me to a standstill. The episodes of dizziness were noted, but not taken seriously until they caused my entire scope of vision to collapse into blackness. I knew that the little sparkly pixels would eventually crowd back into the frame as my vision reassembled. I didn't care that I was acting crazy because I felt alive. And I was not going to let go of that feeling. I would bring it back somehow. It was time to make moves toward a more exciting future.

I am a black-and-white person, so, while I'm fighting to get white, things look okay. But when I am finally at the opposite end of where I started, things get messy.

I kept a hot pink 3x5 card in the desk drawer of my white, wicker desk below the white shutters that opened up to the side yard of my home in Newport Coast. On the card, there was a simple chart: Date, Goal Weight, Weight.

I made the card after several failed attempts to lose twenty pounds. After losing ten, my sister told me I looked emaciated. She was driving me in her black Jetta to the Island to meet Tessa.

"You've lost that sparkle in your eyes, Kali. The thing that made you special, now it's gone," she says, keeping her eyes on the road as we cross over the bridge.

My eyes well up as the statement washes over me the same way the chlorinated water of the high school pool did at five in the morning on an October practice day. I ask her to stop the car and calmly proceed to get out, shut the door, and promise myself to lose forty more.

I'll show you emaciated.

Placing my index fingers below my lower eyelashes, I blot away any remaining teardrops, making sure the comment doesn't also cause a residual mascara failure.

My twisted mind believes that she is right wholeheartedly. But, it also believes that I will be special again if I lose more weight; I will be treasured the way I used to be, the way I was when I was small. Maybe if I try hard enough, if I punish myself sufficiently, I can bring the sparkle that I used to have back into my eyes.

Toward the top of the index card, several rows record weights barely making the two pounds a week lost minimum. Toward the bottom of the index card, many of the columns are blank. I was losing so much weight each week that I was surpassing the goal weight and leaving the column blank altogether. The second to last entry reads: "103."

The latest entry is frightening: "January 4, 2006: 96."

I am five foot six.

I didn't start this process wishing to weigh 96 pounds, but merely to lose two pounds a week until I looked a significant amount skinnier and could fit into the size 00 jeans that I used to fit into with ease. The problem in this equation is that I tend to see things black or white. I'm skinny, or I'm fat. My mind is obsessive in that way. When it came to week three, and I had dropped four pounds, rather than two, I thought I could speed things up by additionally not eating dinner and eating under 400 calories during the day.

It started working. People started commenting. And then, before I knew it, I was throwing up after sessions of eating an entire bag of pretzels, or a healthy amount of my mother's dinner. I didn't want to go back. I didn't want to have to live through the weeks I had struggled, hardly eating a thing. I refused to backtrack. I became obsessed with the feeling of waking up lighter.

Dr. Jane M.D. (GP): September 22, 2006
Chief Complaint: sore throat, cough. Went to urgent care and given z-pack. Fatigue got worse. The patient still goes to school and is doing all activities, including dance. Good appetite.
A/P: strep throat vs. mono??

Nurse: September 26, 2006
Dr. Jane saw this patient. Her mono test came back positive. Thought maybe it shouldn't wait until Wednesday.

Mononucleosis: I Can't Stop

I am now having trouble keeping up at dance rehearsal, and it is starting to show. It has been less than a month since the Prozac experience, but my doctors, parents and I brush it off. I am too busy to think twice about it. The doctor even kept me on a low dose of Prozac for weeks after the incident.

By the end of September, I am diagnosed with mononucleosis after a nurse stumbles upon a positive mono test that my G.P. at the time, Dr. Jane, had overlooked. Dr. Jane had noted that she was debating "strep vs. mono," but it was the nurse who found the test results and brought it to the attention of the other doctor, Dr. Jane's son, Dr. Scott.

I am always tired but chalked it up to not eating enough. And I got sick frequently but felt I had done it to myself, so I didn't seek treatment. It got to a point where I couldn't perform an entire routine at rehearsal without feeling I may very possibly have a heart attack. My body ached. My lungs burned. Mononucleosis, however, was my alibi when anyone, including my parents, asked about my weight.

Academically, I created the perfect storm. I selected all honors and AP classes, along with a zero period (class begins at 7 a.m. and ends at 7:50 a.m.) and an even larger role on the dance team.

I am the historian of Terpsichore this year, and I made both of the dances that the outside, professional choreographer's pieces. It is my Sophomore Year, and I already get to pick the dances I want to be in for the annual show. Underclassmen on the team do not typically get chosen for enough pieces to be able to choose which ones they ultimately want to dance in. On top of that, I auditioned my choreography, and it was picked!

The piece is initially inspired by the lyrics of the song. Over the next few months, it morphs into choreography that tells the story, in real time, of the current struggle.

Terpsichore is scheduled to practice every weekday from 2 p.m. to 7 p.m., but once the pieces for the show start rehearsing days often end at 11 p.m. The length of your rehearsals all depend on how many choreographers choose you for their piece.

I had taken the roller coaster, one tick at a time, all the way up to the top of the track, and it was time to watch inertia do the rest. In my attempt to get my life back under my control, I knocked open the floodgates. "You Don't Have To Do That For Me."

The room is swimming. Are we even in a room? Whose car is this?

"Derrick? Where are we?"

"We're in the Escalade. In front of my house," he says.

"I don't feel good," I say.

"You gonna puke?" Derrick asks.

"I don't know," I say into the side of his jeans. They smell like beer, cigarettes, and cologne, lots of cologne.

"Kali...Kali...Kali! Look at me!"

I'm moving now: being walked into Derrick's house.

Oh hey, Tanner. When did Tanner arrive?

I try to coordinate my walking. I feel like a galloping horse on Somas.

I hope my costume looks good. Do I look skinny at least?

I wake up in Derrick's room, and the rush of nausea sends me running to the bathroom.

I made a commitment to lose weight, and it was only about the second month of the self-devised program. I ran twice a day along with dance rehearsal, having one meal at 2 p.m. and one-fourth of the dinner my mother served. When it came to alcohol, I knew the calorie content could be high. I stuck to vodka and used Diet Coke as a chaser or zero-calorie aspartame-filled water. Of course, I was sick.

I heave my insides into the toilet, only to spew air and nothing else. The pain is insurmountable.

I keep getting stuck in the retching zone for an incredibly long amount of time; the initial kick from your gut that sends you into a possessed state, and you gasp for air as you get a second to take in some oxygen before it happens again. This is the kind of thing where your body hits the physical override mode on your brain's commands.

Your brain says, "Just keep smiling. It will pass."

And your body says, "Great! Thanks for your input, Kali. But I'm going to have to, once again, override your decision to hold it together tonight. Appreciate the feedback."

As the retching gets louder and more desperate, the pain gets stronger. I am throwing up air only to gasp it back into my throat and retch again. My body fights itself.

I am exhausted.

I make the executive decision to help out. I need to get the liquor out of me ASAP. As I stick my hand down my throat, Derrick opens the door. I see his blurry figure standing tall and in the doorway.

"You don't have to do that for me," Derrick says.

The sadness in his words strikes me as he shut the door. It is as if he walked into a situation he wanted to pretend he hadn't.

I search for answers to his statement, but his words echo in my head:

You don't have to do that for me.

You don't have to do that for me.

You don't have to do that for me.

The night falls black again.

From September sixth to December fifth of my Sophomore Year, I lose eighteen pounds. My BMI is eighteen.

Dr. Scott M.D. (GP): December 04, 2006
Add: Mom called, weight loss, told to bring in ASAP

Dr. Scott M.D. (GP): December 05, 2006
Medications: Synthroid
Chief Complaint: weight loss w/mononucleosis.
O: weight loss w/ mononucleosis.
18-pound weight loss since September 06, 2006
BMI 18 right now, W: 111
A/P: Rx Bactrim

Dr. Scott M.D. (GP): December 07, 2006
Add: Patient had reaction to Bactrim, ordered Omnicef

Dr. Scott M.D. (GP): December 26, 2006
Medications: Synthroid
Chief Complaint: sore throat
A/P: strep throat, Rx Augmentin

Dr. Whittman's Trick

I'm starving. I spent the night making my sister a no-egg birthday cake. My boots clack against the cold pavement as I walk away from my mom's BMW. The deserted center looks lonelier than usual. As I swing open Dr. Whittman, my psychologist's, door, the bells on the other side announce my arrival.

Dr. Whittman steps out of his office. He looks even cleaner than normal: his blue plaid dress shirt rolled at the sleeves, and his dark brown slacks freshly ironed. He smiles, looking devious almost, like that guy, who is always showing you the perfect image, transfixed by everything you're saying until you turn your back. I feel this power-hungry vibe from him, but I want to believe in his good side.

He motions toward the sofa right around the corner from the door and takes a seat opposite me on the other coach. I play with my fingers between the ever-expanding gap between my thighs. I try to squeeze them together, but there is a four-inch gap that doesn't budge. My cell phone falls through my legs if I try to hold it there now.

"Have you had an appetite lately?" Dr. Whittman says. He has an unassuming, but intense way about him tonight. Almost as if he is not there: only his body-double.

Holding back the tears welling beneath my eyelids, I am unable to respond. The lump in my throat takes hold of my voice. Dr. Whittman continues, "You seem to have lost a bit of weight, Kali."

He lowers his voice to pronounce my name, and for the first time, I can't answer the second question.

Here it comes. No way to lock this up now.

Tears pour out of my eyes the moment he says my name.

Why did that make me feel so safe?

I controlled my weight in a desperate attempt to make sense out of my life. I used mononucleosis as a disguise to hide my whittling frame. But the secret was out now. I look down at my size 24 True Religion Jeans. They are tattered and patched. They'd been the special "goal" pair from Loehmann's that I had prayed to fit into by Christmas. But Christmas came early and stayed late. Because when I got them, I could barely fit into them. That was less than a couple of weeks ago, and now they fasten easily.

I am proud. And that makes me cry harder.

I cry and plead with the room and cry. I want to go away forever, to be done with everything. I had challenged myself to do this because it was something I could do all of the time. Alcohol had limits (aka parents who were strict), in silent retaliation, I responded with:

Okay, if you won't let me drink, then I just won't eat. I'll show you destructive. Watch me.

But now my mind has been hijacked. And I am through with the insanity.

"I'm so hungry. I'm so hungry, but there are so many rules!" I say, bursting open in Dr. Whittman's office.

I spill my guts to him.

He expresses his concern for my plummeting weight. Not once had Dr. Whittman mentioned my weight before this, not once. He never asked about it. Recently, he had started asking me if I had an appetite, but that's it.

He consoles me for a few minutes with head nods and inspirational statements about taking care of "the vehicle you drive through life with."

Gag

He loved to use this metaphor whenever, and I mean whenever, it only slightly made sense. This time, though, it is put to good use. I actually listen to the story that encompasses the metaphor tonight, and I nod in agreement, "Yes. I get it now."

I am even smiling a tiny bit.

Phew, I feel a little better.

Dr. Whittman excuses himself to use the restroom.

I roll up the damp sleeves of my tie-dyed sweatshirt. I finger-comb my scraggly hair and stretch my tank top over the waistband of my jeans (a nervous thing now that used to be in style). I sniffle until I can breathe again and manage to hold it together long enough to have a cohesive thought.

He comes back about ten minutes later.

I've composed myself and am ready to talk it out.

But he has different plans.

A few minutes later, there's a knock at the office door. I look at it confused as I watch Dr. Whittman calmly get up to open it. My sullen parents appear into the doorframe.

My mother is out of breath, distressed.

"We came as quickly as we could," she says.

"Thank you for coming. Go ahead and take a seat please," Dr. Whittman says, gesturing toward the sofa I'm currently occupying.

Time stops for a moment. It regains momentum after a snapshot is taken of my parents in Dr. Whittman's doorway that would ingrain itself in me. It still sits smack-dab in the middle of my memory's Polaroid wall.

I slide to the far end of the sofa.

I'm speechless. My entire body goes cold.

What about the confidentiality agreement? What about trust? I trusted you! I told you everything. I trusted you. How could you? I told you everything!

The rest of the session is a blur. I sit as far away from my parents as possible. I scoot into the right arm of the sofa, left leg over right, palm to palm, arms jutting into the gap between my thighs. I want nothing to do with what just happened.

My eyes sting from confessing my deepest secrets to the doctor in the minutes prior, maybe it's been an hour. I watch in disbelief and feel myself turning further and further into stone as Gary Whittman offers several multi-colored brochures for different rehab centers.

"You told me you wanted to get away from everything," Dr. Whittman says, noticing that the girl on his sofa is now a stone statue of her once conscious self. I am in shock. Never in my wildest dreams did I think Dr. Whittman would ever trick me like this.

"Not literally!"

By the end of this comment, I am shaking. Shouting.

Everything I trusted, the one thing that I trusted, is bullshit. And now, my worst nightmare is coming true in the most colorful way. I have always been afraid of revealing myself to anybody. I am perpetually afraid of someone actually getting to know me, and it resulting in something bad. I could never pinpoint what I was afraid of specifically, but it's there. And this makes a solid argument for that case. I told Dr. Whittman something private and now look what happened... EXACTLY. And I didn't even choose to tell this third party (aka the people closest to me, aka the people now drained of color, sitting on the therapist's sofa next to me).

    I've turned into a foreigner.

Dr. Scott M.D. (GP): January 11, 2006
Placed in Portofino Rehab for anorexia

My Doctor's Communicated!...Not!

I found the note on the previous page in my general practitioner, Dr. Scott's, file. At least on this occasion my psychologist Dr. Whittman and my general practitioner, Dr. Scott, were in contact. My parents could have also alerted Dr. Scott him. The latter would be more likely.

Meeting Nurse Ratched: The Portofino Rehab Center

I walk into the kitchen. My father, Atticus, is doing the dishes, part of his nightly routine, but tonight, my sister is speaking aggressively to him.

She barely ever comes out of her back bedroom, so this is strange.

The conversation is obviously about me. I know this before my father glances up to see me walk in, cutting Kayla off and causing her to turn around from her lean against the yellow-tiled countertop.

He's drying a plate that is definitely already dry. He throws the damp dishtowel over his shoulder and puts the plate on the tile counter instead of in the dishwasher.

"Kali!" he says.

"I knew you were throwing up! I knew it! I told them. No one believed me," Kayla says.

Congratulations, Kayla.

She presents it as if boasting that tonight was some sort of victory for her. My father says nothing and continues drying the same plate he had in his hands before. He does not react, to her comment. He's usually this way. But he looks up, throwing the dishtowel over his shoulder again and letting the dish hang by his side. His shoulders collapse as he looks at me searching me for answers. He finds nothing there. He rambles off a few questions.

"Do you think you're fat? Because you're obviously not fat...Is it because of dance?" my dad asks.

He pauses to look up from the gaze he fixed a bit to the left of him. I could almost see the mess of thoughts scrambling his mind, desperately trying to place them in a logical order.

"Why? Why? Why were you throwing up?" he says.

My dad shakes his head as if he's left out a crucial step in a rocket-launching mission/neurosurgery with the frustration of someone missing a step when trying to put together Ikea furniture: going backward, step-by-step, yet to no avail.

He tries again: "Is that why it seemed like you were eating so much?"

The next morning, I watch my mother trudge past my open door.

She must be pacing. She stops to look into my room. The dark circles under her eyes stamp themselves in my memory like a photograph negative; so sullen, so tired. She's wearing her faded pink robe, and the pajama set I got her a couple of Mother's Days back. She describes them as "the plaid ones with fruit occasionally." Her favorite pink robe's belt is dragging on the floor next to her slippers. The robe is turning gray, dingy from overuse. The circles under her eyes are caves. I've never seen her like this. She looks like someone in mourning. I guess, in a sense, I had just died to her. The person she thought she knew had died. She mumbles something to me as she looks into my room and sees my eyes open.

Things are gray. Nobody even woke me up for school. It's well past nine a.m. I find as I grab my phone. No new messages, but things have changed. There are no lights on in the hallway. The familiar, dreaded, bright-gray light creeps through the cracks in my shutters. I reach out and open the first set a little more. Yup, overcast. There's a gray layer hanging onto everything.

I pull myself out of bed and make it into the kitchen. I'm greeted with a more down-to-business approach. I am surprised my mom isn't angry. She's more sullen than anything.

"We've scheduled an appointment with a place in San Diego. They can meet you today," she says as she pours herself another cup of coffee and says, "if you are not too sick to be taken there, they will admit you. Otherwise, you will have to stay in the hospital until you gain enough weight to be admitted," she continues talking without looking at me, "I've pulled down two suitcases from the attic."

She has a way of pleading with your soul in a particular tone, soaked in sadness. Her words ooze of this total loss. She's taken this tone with me only a few times prior. And I don't think I'll ever forget each time she did. It was the color of that morning that locked everything in airtight, sealed into my emotional baggage compartment for life.

One of our family friends, Bianca, had heard that I was ill. And seen, actually, since I was now baby-sized. Word gets around like wildfire in Newport, so people took note of my increasingly thin figure, and told their friends.

I had skipped a lot of class and been to several doctors for mono.

It would have been surprising if the ladies weren't bringing it up during one of their morning walks on the Island. Bianca's daughter, Belle, was a year older than me. She also had two sons, one of who was Isaak's age.

I feel both defensive and thankful when the beautifully wrapped box shows up on my doorstep: three new pairs of Juicy sweat suits. That's like $400.00 in comfy sweats. I liked that she had gotten me sweats, smart of her. I was anxious about my clothes not fitting once I gained the weight back.

I envisioned the first real meal adding forty pounds instantly. I had no clue it took work to gain weight back, and that it doesn't come back in the same places. The illness and weight loss had eaten away at my once muscular thighs. Well! At least I have a thigh gap.

Packing List
- 5 pairs of Juicy sweatpants
- 5 hoodies
- UGG slippers (like Dad and Isaak's)
- Derrick's Christmas Card (with the family and their Pomeranian)
- Journal

Abridged for the Reader's Health

I kept a journal throughout the time at Portofino Rehab Center; everything from daily whining to assignments to letters from fellow rehabbers, color the pages. I took the exact words in most cases but deleted most of the writing regarding addiction because I never felt that an eating disorder was my issue. It was something that I dared myself to try when I was told I couldn't drink. I wanted to feel something, so I decided to lose a bunch of weight.

Carol, a marathon-runner, arrived around the same time I got to Portofino. She was one of the women I connected with right away. She was an athlete, around forty, intelligent and a little aloof. I became her "light, " and she was like my mother for the interim period.

Amy checked-in a few days after I did, and it was evident that she was the closest to normal and my age so far. She made everything look cool. Although she had already suffered three heart attacks before arriving to join our group, she was like an older sister. She made everything less serious. I felt like there was a world way bigger than the drama surrounding the rude therapists and insurance company BS when I was with her. She had confidence I would die for, an overly relaxed vibe and could not give a damn what anyone thought of her. I loved it.

Amy drew/painted a picture of me when we were all at a cafe watching a singer/songwriter perform that I've hung on my wall ever since. The thick structured beige paper and the way she made my eyes visibly sparkle with those extra-long lashes remind me of my true self. She also wrote what would become one of my very favorite quotes on the side, telling me to have confidence and shine my light as bright as I can. She marked the quote as a Nelson Mandela quote, and to this day I thought it was until I searched it again and found it is actually a Marianne Williamson quote.

The Portofino Journal

Day 1: January 15, 2007

Joy is a simple thing that we all deserve to feel, yet it often slips away from us while we are too caught up in our busy lives to slow down. We forget it's there after a while.

Love: I never seem to acknowledge it until it's ripped away. I distance myself so far away from people it seems quite impossible for there to be any true love involved. I spend my days frantically making sure I am not emotionally attached to anyone so that if it were all stolen away from me, I would be okay.

All these thoughts and strategies seem to have been put to death now that I am here. If I end up in the same destination, alone anyway, it's probably better not to be lonely when I'm around the people I love. XO Kali Rae

Day 2: January 16, 2007

I don't relate to anyone here. It's hard to listen to their chatter about things that will only make them worse. I am at the point where I do not care what I have to do. I just want to go home. I've told every therapist that I will do literally anything to be able to go home. Hopefully, they realize how far I am along with getting better. I truly feel that my eating disorder is gone because I realized the things that caused it and know now to stop it before it takes over. I just want to go home, and yet no one else here seems to share this wish. I don't understand.

The girls keep talking about how there is a thirty-day minimum. There is NO WAY. And the aid joined in tonight with condescending laughter, irritated by her uselessness (because I said I didn't need help and never do because I don't have an issue with food): "Wow, you seem to be plodding along! You don't any indication to be having any problems. I'd slow down if I were you." She laughs and turns back to talk to Amanda (the girl who's been here for thirteen months and constantly says that she will never get better and there is no way you can make her go home. Uhmmm?)

She is an ex-pre-Olympic gymnast with frizzy hair, always in two balls of pigtails on the top of her head. She resembles a chipmunk due to the incessant bulimia that caused her glands to swell up. She wears her issues as a badge of honor. And she is our resident mean girl. She hates me, and it's apparent to everyone. But no one here likes me, so, nothing new.

Rolling her eyes, Amanda threw down her utensils after the comment about me, and screamed at the top of her lungs,

"Why are you even here?"

She stomped away from the table and up the stairs. Sarah and the two other girls my age made their own comments before following Amanda upstairs.

I feel out of place and awkward when I easily finish my meals, and other girls can't get past the first bite. Get me out of here! I'll do whatever I need to do. Just get me out! This isn't the place for me. I am becoming way more depressed. All these girls talk about is how much we're eating and how it will make them fat.

Honestly, I've never thought I was fat. I don't think I'm fat. And like I've said a million times, I DID THIS AS AN EXPERIMENT.

I was angry with how confused and out of place I felt in the world and especially under the watchful eye of my parents and decided that instead of drinking I would stick it to them but refusing to eat. It was a tool to be an asshole. I was being stubborn, and then it got exhilarating, and now I'm here.

But, I got it. It's not something you mess with; however, I still don't have a problem with my weight or food. I have a crawling out of my skin-bored problem. This was a test of willpower, and now I'm imprisoned and being made to feel extremely guilty for NOT having a problem with eating. I have enough problems. Guys, you have got to trust me on this. This just isn't it. Sorry.

Later...

I walked in on Amanda and Sarah discussing techniques for throwing up when they lost their gag reflex. I also learned that one of my favorite artists, Fiona Apple, was a part of this worldwide anorexia gang that wore red bracelets and other symbols. And the girls say that they share information online about how not to eat.

News to me! It's like a gang. They both had to have their bracelets cut off after being admitted, I guess, and their phones wiped due to their "secret accountability buddies." WHAT! It's an anorexia gang; they have secret messaging groups online too. XO Kali Rae

Day 3: January 17, 2007

I just got off the phone with my mom, and I am inconsolable.

Is this a sick movie?

I was trying to tell my mom how I was feeling and Christy hung up on her. She cut off the call and then calmly, robot-like told me that I was not allowed to discuss my treatment. It had only been three minutes! I fucking hate them.

They just want to keep me here to make money off me. Even the girls here won't stop reminding me of the thirty-day minimum, which is complete bullshit. I get to come home on Saturday, so I only have to wait a couple more days...but, now, it feels like the staff holds something against me because of the phone call. They are treating me very weird. I am a complete outsider here. I feel like I am in some sort of movie where they trap you in rehab.

A runner came today. She's probably around fifty, and I like her a lot. She's struggling badly, though. She's refusing to finish her meals, the carefully portioned one dairy one fat one protein, etc. Not calorie-based. "Calorie" is like the N-word here. You must finish everything they feed you and by everything, I mean; we are talking, drops of orange juice here. Things have to be licked clean, or you are given either;

    A. Regular Ensure (if twenty percent of the meal is not finished)

    B. Two Regular Ensures (if thirty percent of the meal is unfinished), or the worst,

    C. Three double Ensures.

Most people puke when they are forced to do this and in response are forced to start all over again.

Also, we were not allowed to leave the table without finishing. Almost every meal I finish and have to sit at the table and watch as one, then two and then several staff members came to the table to coax Eleanor, Amanda, and Carol to finish their assigned Ensures. Instead of coaching the women, the therapists would just threaten them. And when Eleanor had to puke, they followed her and told her she was stronger than that.

We aren't ever allowed to close the bathroom doors completely, so I heard everything, all the time. It's hard always to be the one scarfing down every meal and snack no problem, when everyone else at the table is throwing tantrums, puking or crying. I have been eating Amanda, Sarah and Carol's brownie bites for them. It's a serious operation that would result in another month of treatment for all of us if caught, but I'll take my chances. Amanda has been here so long that she's basically mapped the tendencies of each of the staff members, including Christy. I don't pay attention really until I feel a lumpy napkin in my lap; the brownie wrapped up. I'd then study the on-call staff member until I saw them look away to console one of the sobbing women. At that point, I stuff all three brownie bites into my mouth, swiftly removing them from the napkin. No one says a word, but Carol looks up from her feet, her shoulders hunched over her plate, just for a moment, to smile at me.

Only two more days here...You can do this.

Just breathe.

Carol told me later that I make everything easier and thanked me. I feel bad for the cook. Everyone thinking and to the table when it's mealtime and then either picks the food apart and makes rude comments about it (Amanda) or says, "I can't do this," and starts crying...just a couple of examples. Her portabella mushroom literally made me wretch; good thing it was silent, or I would have been marked as needing to stay longer. But it was huge and rubbery and tasted like YUCK! Tough crowd. Dinner will be interesting again tonight. They will all probably make smart ass comments about me as I scarf down my food. Am I crazy or is it normal to eat what's on your plate? Ya, I think it's freaking normal! Aaaaaah...get me out of this cage. XO Kali Rae

Day 4: January 18, 2007

It is very frustrating to keep hearing the phrase, "Don't quit before the miracle happens." I get it; you don't think my miracle happened...cool, bro. The miracle can happen the first day you get here or the thirty-first day after you get here.

If one more therapist asks me how I am doing and then says I am wrong, I will run away. I say I am not having any problems with eating and they say, "Well we're going to have to work on that."

You don't know me. I have other problems, but that's not one of them. I have no one to talk to about how I actually feel. No one is listening!! HELP!

I know God has given me the miracle of recovery. No one can tell me otherwise: no one, not Amber, not Christy, not the mean dietician. Please let me talk to someone. I'll do anything—actually, not anything. I will not stay here longer. I'd rather kill myself.

Breaking News! Eleanor is puking for the third time since I've been here. She pukes up her food because her body can't handle it anymore. She's about sixty I think. XO Kali Rae

Day 5: January 19, 2007

It's Friday! That means I can probably make it until Saturday. I'm stoked, and I'm also really excited to go out to lunch today. TGI Fridays!
Everyone is scared because we can't order diet soda or just eat water. Lol. Oh, and you aren't allowed to order salad for dinner. I'm excited to go to a restaurant! We went to the beach yesterday, and the smell was comforting. Later that night, the cook's husband came over to fix a light. Even though we weren't allowed to talk to him or even be in the same room as him, it felt good to know he was there.

A little later...
Eleanor made it through dinner without puking. That's basically incredible for her... Tomorrow I get picked up before twelve o'clock I am so excited to get out of here. Today is my fifth day... Wow!
House Meeting:
Mindfulness: No longer live a back in a sort of deep sleep and let my addictions take over my life, not eating, not drinking and not drugs! They will not control my life. I can now cross eating off that list completely, and that is very relieving. I don't have a problem with drugs so that can be crossed off, leaving only one thing... Alcohol.
I'm not ready to erase that from the list, yet but I'm ready to say that it will not run my life. I make all the decisions around here. I make them all.
I've also become aware of all that the things I take for granted in my life. The things that truly mean the most to me are overlooked each and every day. It's funny how those things work out. The things in my life that mean the most are the things least appreciated by myself. It makes no sense. No sense at all. Life is so contradicting. It mocks itself. No wonder it's so difficult to be a part of it. By the way, Carol says that she truly sees that I do not have eating disorder problems and notices the comments like, "You'll hit a bump in the road sometime," offend me greatly. XO Kali Rae

Day 6: January 20, 2007

I broke down sobbing twice last night after a phone call with my mom. Carol, once again, was able to comfort me and reassure me. My mom talked to the staff, and they said I was doing "pretty well." What the hell? I and every other person here, including the staff, know that I'm doing so much better than "pretty well."

I am extremely upset about having to stay another week. It is so unnecessary for me to be here. Carol told me it was obvious that every staff member realizes how out of place I am. She says it probably has to be about insurance. It's protocol to say "pretty well" after the first week since you have to stay for two weeks for insurance to cover it. Sherry added that if you leave after the first week, then you just never had to be there in the first place.

At the restaurant yesterday, I was the only one not feeling like we're going to a slaughterhouse; three were crying, and one got sick. I ordered milk just for kicks and one extra dairy! That's a new one.
XO Kali Rae

Day 7: January 21, 2007

I'm back in hell. Everything is really tense around here right now. They had to put Eleanor back in the hospital tonight, and nobody thinks she will make it. Carol is freaking and seriously thinking about leaving after having an argument with Christy regarding the fat intake and their system of measuring for our food plans. Carol thought it was ridiculous that the fettuccine Alfredo only counted as one carb, one fat, and one dairy when it could have served four of each of us. I agree with this, but Christy isn't smart enough or educated enough to understand the legitimacy of what Carol is saying. Plus, Amanda tried to throw up her dinner tonight. Sarah and I caught her after we heard the door slam, against house rules, upstairs.

We aren't allowed to close the doors to the bathroom. So, we have to have a "spotter" outside the door every time we need to use the restroom. AKA, you are screwed if you are shy. We ran up to find Amanda disheveled, and Sarah had to pull Amanda's hand out of her throat. She was hunched over the toilet. XO Kali Rae

Day 8: January 22, 2007

It's Amy's twenty-fifth B-Day! She's the best. She is the only person I can talk to like a regular person. She was checked in here after having her third heart attack. She's a kindergarten teacher, artist, and writer. She smokes cigarettes outside the back door and makes it look cool.
XO Kali Rae

Day 9: January 23, 2007

Yesterday was a pretty good day. A binge-eater checked in, just what I had hoped would be the next addition. She is a jovial elementary school teacher who can finish four pizzas in one sitting. I'm still little nervous about my parents with having to check me out of this place. I just have to keep the faith.

House Meeting:
Step One: I have used the eating disorder and alcohol to "numb out" of my life's problems. Instead of dealing with emotions that need to be dealt with, I stuff them down and the ED and alcohol gave me something to focus on. These things badly affected me in a variety of ways...

Physically – I was too weak to think or move; too tired to do things I've always loved doing, felt horrible a lot of the time, and my body was failing.

Emotionally – I wasn't feeling any emotions really. At times, I feel very guilty. I was lying to myself and others, and feeling confused and angry. I was not me most of the time. I felt lonely and I was very distant.

Spiritually – I had no spirituality whatsoever, and that is not me.

Socially – I just wasn't myself...

Later...
Anxiety grows about getting out of here. My parents told me to have faith, but I'm extremely scared. XO Kali Rae

Day 10: January 24, 2007

I know now that I can't lie to myself about how I'm treating my body. My body is a vehicle, and without proper care, it will be wasted. Like Whittman says, "Your body is like a fancy car to drive your soul around in." So basically, if I don't take care of it, I won't have a classy way of arriving at point B. XO Kali Rae

Day 12: January 26, 2007

I've made the decision to stop drinking for now. This is the first, and last time I'll be crippled by something outside of myself. I am not sure Derrick is going to support my decision. If he doesn't, I will leave. I need to be selfish. I am worth it. XO Kali Rae

Day 13: January 27, 2007

I'm getting picked up at 3:30 today! I really want to take the mood stabilizer the psychiatrist prescribed for me. So, I'll bring it up. I'm also really excited to have a dietitian, therapist, and psychiatrist. I am also going to attend some meetings. I went to Alcoholics Anonymous (AA) and Narcotics Anonymous (NA) with Amy after she arrived, and found that I fit in there way better. But I agreed to go to Overeaters Anonymous (OA) and Eating Disorders Anonymous (EDA) meetings as well. XO Kali Rae

January 28, 2007

I'm home! Thank God. I have a couple of assessments with two different people tomorrow. I hope they're easy because I am tired of telling people how I feel. XO Kali Rae

January 30, 2007

I haven't written any music lately. It's been hard to keep my thoughts together. My brain feels like Gumby. XO Kali Rae

A Doggy Bag of Prescription Samples and a Hawaiian T-Shirt

Portofino suggested a psychologist, psychiatrist, and a dietician. I got all three after a short trial process to get to know the doctors. I settled on a psychiatrist pretty quickly. His name is Dr. Morano. My father accompanies me to my first visit with him after a very long day the day prior, visiting different psychologists.

The office is bigger than I imagined. The patient files that the front desk has to sort through is literally, walls deep. The multi-color folders lining the bookcase looking shelving units behind the receptionist look like something out of *Harry Potter.*

My dad is irritated.

"He's a Trojan," he says. He never came with me to doctor's appointments like this, but my mom was busy, so here he is in the exam room with me.

"Kali," My dad looks at me in all seriousness and repeats, "He's a Trojan. I don't trust him."

He is slightly joking.

Speaking of the devil...

A jolly-looking man enters wearing, no joke, a USC-themed Hawaiian button-up shirt. He outstretches his arm energetically to present a firm handshake. I am surprised my father doesn't comment.

"Hi. How are yah? A Trojan I see," my dad says.

"I was a UCLA undergrad. I go both ways," Dr. Morano responds.

"How could you?" My dad mocks a surprised demeanor but is obviously happier.

"So, how are you, Kali?" the doctor asks as I adjust myself on the crinkling paper.

"I'm good. Thanks. How are you?" Ignoring my courtesy check, he whips his head back down to my chart.

Don't ask about my weight. Don't ask about my weight. Don't ask about my weight.

"I've talked a little bit with the doctors over at Portofino." He looks up as he flips the top sheet over the clipboard. "I have a couple of things to make your life a little bit easier. What do you think about that?" He says this and looks up, catching my gaze, but I'm confused. "Are you ready to feel better!" he asks.

It's like he's riling up a two-year-old, but I don't hate it. His playfulness is relaxing. I miss having fun, people laughing with me, cheering me up.

"I'm down," I say.

"One thing, it doesn't say here, so I have to ask. Are you actively throwing up?"

"No."

"Great! We will start you on Wellbutrin. Also, I have a few samples of Seroquel. It should help you get to sleep. And I'll put Lyrica in there too; it should help you with pain. I saw that on your chart. Oh, and Wellbutrin will give you seizures if you do throw up. That's why I asked."

He shakes both our hands and my father and him share another USC/UCLA joke as he exits.

"It was great to meet both of you!"

Could it be this easy? Is this all not my fault? Doesn't he hate me?

A nurse enters and shells out the prescriptions, one at a time.

"Okay, so we've got these two and these as well."

She hands me a shiny, plastic Pfizer bag stuffed with little boxes of trial Seroquel, Wellbutrin, and Lyrica. A couple of sample boxes are popped open: the seals are broken. She sees them, removes them, checks the content, and folds that top back into itself. She then hands me a reminder card.

"If this time doesn't work, just let the front desk know."

"My wife will be here next time," My dad says, unnecessarily. I can tell he feels awkward.

On my next visit to Dr. Morano, he prescribes Lamictal to "stabilize" my mood. I say I'm feeling more anxious than usual.

Dr. Morano looks up from his clipboard. "That's normal," he says.

"Really?" I ask.

"Here's what I'll do..." Dr. Morano explains that this next drug should help me with the anxiety. He disregards the idea that the

Wellbutrin may have been the cause. His gaze is so sincere it's almost crazed. He is so sure of himself as he scribbles down the indecipherable notes.

Reflections on Meeting Dr. Morano

The first drug-pusher I visited signed a copy of his brand new book and sent me home with a doggy bag of prescription samples. The bag' contents would change each time, but I'd always leave his office with samples of something new.

Although I was unaware of how oddly I was acting while on these medications, my mother watched me like a hawk and reported back to the doctors what had gone down in the weeks following the new meds. I was put on medications whose side effects always had a more devastating outcome than a positive shift in my mood and behavior most of the time. I acted normal in most situations but would resort to precarious behavior when no one was watching.

Bridges that I saw over water would evoke a voice that said, "Jump! Do it!" followed by a rush of adrenaline to carry the plan out. If I didn't take action, I'd get the stream of unworthiness comments:

You are a burden. No one wants to deal with you anymore. Your sister would be so much happier, and your parents' marriage would be great if you just weren't here anymore.

And then new adrenaline would surge through my veins. Adrenaline-laced with martyrdom that told me everyone would be so much better without me around. And I would, quite literally, jump off the bridge. I did jump off of bridges. I remember the Lido Bridge vividly. I swam like crazy to get to the dock so that I could run back up to the bridge and grab my bike. My friend shrieked behind me, "Cops!" as I pedaled faster.

Anything that seemed unnecessary or dangerous to try, I wanted to try. Nothing, not one ounce of energy in my body, told me to take a breath and weigh my options. I did not consider options. I weighed exhilaration and feeling alive vs. feeling dead inside. I was impulsive and one-track minded. I just wanted to feel.

Dr. Morano M.D. (psychiatrist): February 02, 2007
Samples of Seroquel, Wellbutrin, and Lyrica

Unknown Number

Unknown: Happy Valentine's Day Kali -Jaxx Moreau

What? I don't remember giving him my number. My heart skips a beat as I text back. It's refreshing to feel good.

Me: Happy Valentine's Day Jaxx!
Jaxx: Has it been romantic?
Me: Nope, you?
Jaxx: Wanna be my Valentine?
Me: Always :)

The Boys' Dance, Keg-Stands, and Choices

It is March of Sophomore Year, and I am taking the first samples that the new doctor, Dr. Morano, threw my way. These samples include; Wellbutrin, Seroquel, and Lyrica. Simultaneously, I'm trying to stumble gracefully into the new quarter of school. I'd missed about two months of school if I add in the days off here and there when the illness began.

Terpsichore just finished their third night of performances. However, due to the absences and sickness before January's hospitalization, I had to pull out of dancing in the show. I'm watching from the wings. The dances I choreographed and co-choreographed are still performed. However, other dancers fill the coveted spots I snatched in the guest choreographer's pieces: the ideal placement I had worked so many years to be given and was still surprised by, also, carefully covered up. The dances were re-staged for a performance minus one dancer.

It was difficult to watch tonight, but I am very proud of the dance that I choreographed. The final piece is a dance with great emotional depth.

The theme of the dance is insanity. It focuses on one girl who is not wearing a "straitjacket" (a backward, white ballet sweater). This girl is seen tweaking out, "crazy," in comparison to the other dancers who are in sync. After some time, two more mentally ill soloists join her from offstage. By the end, the sane majority overtakes all three dancers. This is demonstrated by the tying up of the straitjacket around each of the insane dancers as the lights dim. The music is brooding: haunting in its carefully crafted anticipatory sound that at no point finds a climax, placed atop a bass line like a slow, steady heartbeat pulsing throughout.

One of the dancer's fathers, whom I had never spoken to, pulled me aside after the first night's show to tell me that my piece brought him to tears. Another dad, the father of one of the dancers that my sister and I grew up with, told me that it was the best dance he had ever seen, and that he'd seen a lot of dances following Ashley to her competitions every weekend for the past ten years.

It is a piece that speaks directly from my heart. It ends up being a glimpse into a dark autobiography. I hadn't set out to do this, but as life would have it, watching the piece, I feel my hairs stand on end. The dance is a mirror of what is happening in my life.

I feel I am running away from a constant barrage of people telling me what is right and what is crazy, only to find myself more out of sorts than before. I simply looked more pulled together from the outside.

I smile politely as I watch the handsome group of senior boys strut back onto the stage. I finally get to do something, though, because it's time for bows. Hence why the boys are backstage. It's time for them to take their well-rehearsed bows in front of the hundreds of students and parents filling the local college's theater.

I feel a pang of embarrassment as I am reminded that I am still not in dance clothes.

I carefully chose my outfit; ripped jeans (the light-colored Seven Jeans, that distressed with a cheese-grater, paying particular attention to the left side to make them look naturally worn) and a new, navy-blue sweater. The sweater doesn't look nonchalant, classy like I planned it to anymore. Under the bright spotlights of the stage, it looks dull like someone threw it into their pile of clothes "to donate" and I had fished it out.

I walk to the middle wing feeling uncomfortable, knowing I am about to announce my failure-of-a-self to the auditorium.

"And our sophomores!" Melinda announces, her voice booming through the microphone.

The cheers roar. I walk out behind the three other girls. The stage lights are familiar, but my tall black boots are extra hot. I'm used to slip-on jazz shoes and tights, not jeans and boots. I smile awkwardly and walk. The other girls are already waiting in formation. I clasp hands with my best dance friend, Raquel. She squeezes my hand and smiles warmly. Thank God for her.

The bows are choreographed, so I thankfully begin to lose my thoughts in the sway of the clapping and bobbing.

As Kayla and I leave the auditorium, one of the Senior boys shouts to us, "You both coming tonight?"

Before Kayla can answer, the Senior boy's friend chimes in, "Kali should come, Kay!"

"Yeah, bring Kali," a third Senior boy teases Kayla about the after party.

"Oh ya?" Kayla says.

Of course, I'm coming. I choreographed that last dance. I'm the best sophomore on the team.

Okay. Whoa. Check yourself, Woman.

As I walk through the Newport Coast home, the smell of liquor and cologne is strong. It's not long before I am downing red cups full of beer from the keg. Two Senior boys assist me in my first real keg-stand, lifting me up by the ankles; my shirt almost falls up over my head. Raquel catches it and tucks it into my jeans. At least, you did the skinny thing right. Kali. Well done.

The bland, cold beer rushes down my throat. The elixir makes my heart race immediately.

Damn! I miss this stuff.

Moments later, I am blurry. My sense of time and space vanished, but I am still conscious. And, I'm still talking.

"Blaise and Kelly want to hook up with you," Ashley says, she's holding my shoulders like a wrestling coach before they send their wrestler into the ring. Ashley is the co-president of the dance team with my sister. She has lived down the street from me my entire life. Ashley is sweeter than humanly possible. So, this is interesting coming from her. "So who do you choose?" Ashley asks.

I get a wave of the "I've been chosen!" feeling: the kind of feeling that lights you up, energizing every inch of your body with fresh blood, bursting you out of the mundane into the creation zones. You are again reminded of your own worth, by the simple acknowledgment that someone chooses you.

Later that night, a tall, tan water polo player approaches me. I know his face from early morning practice in the pool. Kelly is a star player, supposedly brilliant, an all-around good guy. He is off to Harvard in the fall.

I feel weird knowing about his life, but I was told I should meet him at one point, and it all comes rushing to the forefront of my mind.

Kelly walks right up to me. He places his hand on the wall above my head as a sort of kickstand before bringing his face pretty close to mine. He places his other hand on my hip.

His eyes are soft. He has a boyish look about him; big brown eyes, his hair swooped across his forehead, bleached from the sun and messy.

Suddenly the door to a room bursts open as Kelly presses me through it. He pushes me over to the bed in the dark and closes the door. I can't see anything.

And then, he is on top of me. My feet aren't touching the ground. am on my back.

I am physically there, but I am gone.

I blackout. (See Appendix C.)

I wake up in the hallway under a bright light. Kelly is leaning against the opposite wall. Several other people are around drinking out of red cups.

Was it a dream?

I can tell by the way Kelly keeps looking over my way that it wasn't.

Kayla approaches me. She seems pissed.

Why?

"Let's go home," Kayla says quickly.

"No, don't go yet!" Kelly says. He swings his arm around my neck. "Let Kali stay…Pleeeease Kay Kay?"

"Oh God." Kayla rolls her eyes. "Kali, we are leaving now. Okay?"

"Kayla, seriously, let her stay with me." Kelly pleads as I melt.

"Whatever," Kayla says. She walks away as Ashley approaches.

"Kayla is so mad," Ashley says. I can tell by Ashley's face that she feels guilty.

"What? Why?" I ask.

"I'm sorry. I didn't know. I guess Kayla was sort of into Kelly," Ashley says.

"What? She has a boyfriend!" I say.

"Whoa, whoa, ladies, relax. This isn't about Kayla," Kelly interrupts.

"She's my sister!" I say.

"Her sister!" Ashley interrupts, echoing me, "Of course it's about her, Kelly!"

Dr. Morano M.D. (psychiatrist): March 15, 2007
Added Lamictal
Samples of Abilify*
*Dr. Morano doesn't note that I am already taking Seroquel, Lyrica, and Wellbutrin. He adds a sample of Abilify to cure the daily migraines. He also thinks it will help with my mood. (See Appendix K.)

Spring Break: Palm Desert with the Terpsichore Girls

It's Spring Break and like years prior, I'm heading to the Marriott Desert Springs Hotel in Palm Springs. It is the first time I will be there on my own, sans parents.

My parents sometimes rent a villa for themselves and allow us to stay in a separate one with our friends. There is enormous pressure to do this. Kids expect their parents to book villas for them as well stock said Villa with a plethora of alcohol and unlimited beer, and provide the cash to spend on $12 daiquiris to spike with the flask stuffed in your Michael Kors tote.

My ex-boyfriend, Derrick, will most certainly be there, probably with his private villa, possibly two, but I am more excited than worried. I am staying with older Terpsichore girls, and therefore, older guys. Derrick should be no problem at all.

"Will you come throw up with me?" Lana asks, snatching me out of my daydream as I wait for a drink at the poolside bar. She motions toward the tiled-restroom entrance.

"What?" I ask her confused.

"I ate this gross quesadilla," Lana continues, eyes ablaze, "and you look really good, like really skinny. How did you do it?"

Is she really...is she making fun of me right now?

"Yeah, I've been sick. But, no, sorry, I don't do that," I say.

She grabs my hand, pulling me into the restroom behind her.

"You're funny!" she says. Lana undoes her shorts before slamming open the door to the bathroom.

"So like, how are you?" she asks from the toilet.

What. The. Fuck.

I had been told that this girl didn't like me because of Derrick, but this is weird.

"I heard you broke up with Derrick. Are you okay?" Lana asks.

"Well...yeah—," before I can continue, she pushes, forcefully, out of the stall, stumbling, trying to button her denim shorts (which is not happening for her).

I watch as she gives up, unzips them, and rolls them down exposing her fuchsia bikini bottoms.

"I'm fat," she whines.

"Oh god. Really?" I say.

Scooping up my hand once again, Lana pulls me out of the bathroom laughing, "Let's get a drink...I have LOTS of liquor!"

She barks an order at the bartender who is all of the twenty-five...maybe.

"Two piña coladas! Pronto, Buddy!" Lana says, turning to me, "I've got this." She whips out her credit card.

"You have ID?" The sandy-blonde bartender asks.

"No," Lana says.

"Virgin it is," the bartender says.

"Dude. Whatever," Lana says, and swings the two beverages around, giving one to me.

"Thank you!" I say.

I chug half of the drink. I knew the drill: drink a quarter of the glass to make room for the liquor, and do it fast and without a word about it.

"Anytime. Here, let me do it," Lana says.

She unscrews the cap of the little Absolute bottle she has in her purse and pours more than enough into my plastic Marriott cup.

"So like who do you want to hook up with?" she asks.

I am still stuck on her initial question.

Dr. Morano M.D. (psychiatrist): April 19, 2007
Seroquel increased to 100mg
Lamictal increased to 200mg
Stopped Abilify
Samples of Wellbutrin XL tried again at 150mg

Dose Switching in May

A week after the Spring Break trip, Dr. Morano increases the Seroquel to 100mg and the Lamictal to 200 mg. He doesn't state the reasons or record the samples he gave me at the last appointment.

The Wellbutrin, as decided by my mother, made me crabby, but I was to try it one more time. The Abilify gave me one of the worst migraines I ever had. I discontinued it without approval. Dr. Morano never asked about it.

By May, I am coming back off of Wellbutrin. Dr. Morano notes Wellbutrin "again wasn't tolerated at 150mg." (See Appendix G.)

I am also decreasing the Lamictal by half, as well as the Seroquel. Seroquel is giving me nighttime carbohydrate cravings and bad headaches in the morning. (See Appendix I.)

Topamax is added in May to help with the headaches. Dr. Morano notes he starts me on Topamax "low and slow." (See Appendix Q).

He notes to himself to "consider another atypical" as well as "consider another GABA agent."

After all of this dosage switching, medication swapping, and combining, Dr. Morano requests a follow-up a month later. He notes that I should probably discontinue Seroquel but is waiting to see how I react to lowering it first.

> Dr. Morano M.D. (psychiatrist): May 14, 2007*
> Medications: Synthroid, Seroquel 50mg, Lamictal 100mg, Wellbutrin XL 150mg
> S: Decreased the Seroquel from 100 to 50mg—less spaciness but doesn't sleep as well.
> Wellbutrin XL—again wasn't tolerated at 150 mg dose.
> Decreasing Lamictal from 200mg down to 100 mg—no obvious difference was seen and thinks that looking back 100mg was the best dose in comparison even at 50mg when she started to see positive results. Didn't take Seroquel one night and didn't sleep well all night. Patient has headaches off and on. Cravings P.M. (See Appendix I.)
> A/P: I'll continue Lamictal 100mg. I'll add Topamax low and slow. Consider decrease or D/C Seroquel depending on results seen. Consider another atypical. Consider other GABA agent.
> F/U in about 3-4 weeks or sooner

*This is the only time that Dr. Morano typed out his notes. The format is drastically different than his usual couple of words scrawled across the lined page.

Sixteen Candles, a Goldfish, and a Range Rover

"**I**'ve got food!" my mom shouts down the hallway to my room. I run out of my room to see what she's got. She is coming through the front door carrying huge bags of California Pizza Kitchen.

"My favorite food ever! Did you get the pizza too?" I ask.

"Of course I did," my mom says.

"Ah! Mom! You are the best!" I say. My phone dings:

Tessa: Do you have alcohol?

That's slightly annoying, but logical, I guess. I put the phone down without answering, so I can help unpack the food. My phone dings again. It's the same text again.

Me: I'm sure the guys will bring some.

Tessa: Want to just meet me at Trey's?

Me: No, come over. My Mom got food and everything.

Tessa: Okay :)

I look up from the phone, as my mom is bringing in pie tins out of the freezer. She sets them on the bar.

"Great idea to make frozen yogurt pie, Kali," my mom says.

"Thanks!"

My heart aches a little thinking about how special my mom is making this party for me, aware that the kids will just want alcohol.

My brother's girlfriend, Kara, shows up first. She's carrying a big pink bag: "Sprinkles cupcakes."

"Kara! You got Sprinkles!" I shout. (These cupcakes cost $4 each and taste like it too. They were so sought after people traveled to Newport to buy them.)

Behind her, I catch a glimpse of my new car parked out front: a white Range Rover Sport.

"I saw your car!" Kara says, "You got a Range!"

"I know. I can't even believe it's mine," I say.

"Kara!" My mom shouts, coming around the corner to greet her, "Oh! You are too sweet." My mom grabs the designer cupcakes, hugging Kara like a long-lost child.

By 7 p.m., carloads of people are showing up at my door, not house-party amounts; the party is invite-only. Not too many, especially since we weren't serving alcohol. The boys show up as the sun is setting, sans my boyfriend, Blaise.

Drew, a good friend of mine, arrives with a goldfish in one hand, and two-fifths of Smirnoff in the other; the necks of the bottles strangled by his grasping fingers.

Blaise never shows.

By 8 p.m., we are at Trey's, drinking. I black out after roaming Trey's with the two bottles in hand: watermelon Smirnoff in one, green apple Smirnoff in the other. The bottles are empty by the end of the night, and I am too. (See Appendix C.)

I open my eyes, and I am at a slant. I must be leaning against the door. I hear Blaise's voice from the passenger seat in front of me:

"Well, I'm not taking her home," Blaise says.

"We can just kind of drop her on the porch," the female voice of the driver responds.

"Screw you guys. Drive her to Kayla's. I'll bring her in," another voice says.

"Oh my God! Atticus!" my mom's voice is far off, "Isaak! Atticus!"

Moments later, I feel myself handed from one person's arms to another's: my fathers.

"I'm so sorry," the unfamiliar voice says.

Who is that?

"Did she take anything?" my father is calm, drawing on his summers spent as a California State Lifeguard.

"I don't know. I wasn't with her," the voice from the car says.

"Who was?" my dad asks.

Who is that?

"I don't know," he responds.

The bright lights of my parents' kitchen are blazing. Upon waking up, I heave into the yellow puke bowl from the kitchen. My mother is next to me. My father tries to calm her down. "Michelle, we can't take her to the hospital now. The only thing they will be able to do is put saline in her. She needs to metabolize the alcohol," my dad says. He comes over to me, "Kali we need to take a walk, okay?"

"No," I heave again.

"We're going for a walk. You aren't throwing up anything anymore. We've got to get the alcohol out of your system."

He hands me a water bottle. I refuse it.

I come to again, and we are at the end of my street. My arm is draped around my father's neck.

"I want to go home," I moan. Even the darkness is nauseating.

"We can't do that yet, Kali. One more time around the block."

Seroquel'd in Public, More Specifically, in Maui

My parents and I are in Maui for Memorial Day weekend to celebrate a family friend's wedding. We just finished dinner. It's the perfect temperature outside, warm but not hot. The sun just went down. The breeze catches the palm trees and they sway. I watch them from our balcony above.

"Haaayy-aay!" Bon Jovi's voice echoes through the buildings of the Marriott Hotel in Maui. The music wafts through the sand-covered path leading back to the hotel lobby.

"Wait a second, is that Bon Jovi?" I hear my father's voice faintly from the inside of the hotel room. I am on the balcony that spans the entire suite.

"Dad! I think Bon Jovi is playing!" I shout back into the room.

My mom is cranky.

"Come on guys. I've got to go to bed," she says from the bed.

"Dad! Let's go down there!" I yell. "He must be playing on the beach. It sounds pretty close."

"Why didn't we hear it coming back from dinner?" my dad asks.

"Let's go!" I say and slam the glass door to the balcony.

"Okay, Let's go!" my dad says, "Michelle, please come with us."

"No!" she shouts, angry now.

We laugh.

"Okay, Hon," my dad says.

Shit, a drunken haze begins to fall over my body. Shit. Shit. Shit. I already took the Seroquel.

I think back to my last appointment with Dr. Morano.

Dr. Morano reminds me each time he up's the Seroquel dosage, "Make sure you are in bed when you take this."

"I sleep," I report, a bit uneasy, "Sometimes I feel like I can't breathe because I'm so tired."

"That's normal. Make sure you drink a full glass of water with it. So good to see you doing better!" Dr. Morano responds. He shakes my hand.

"Let's keep you right on track here," he says. He wraps up each of the visits this way. Then he smiles like a clown and exits. One afternoon he pops his head back into the room.

"My book is coming out soon. I'll sign it for yah no problem!"

"Yeah? Oh wow, how exciting," my mother says. "A book, huh?"

She looks over at me. I catch her sarcasm, but Dr. Morano certainly doesn't. My mom turns to me, "Kali, you should write a book," she says.

Flashback to Maui and Bon Jovi, my dad and I have been walking for several minutes down the sandy path leading us from the hotel lobby out to the other buildings of the resort, and the beach.

We finally make it to a green fence lining the makeshift venue enclosing the Bon Jovi resort. We have been trying to find ways to either get inside the fence or see above it.

"I didn't know you liked Bon Jovi!" my dad says enthusiastically.

Shit. My dad doesn't know what happens. Shit. I've got to leave like fifteen minutes ago.

I try to speak, but my mouth feels numb.

"I've gotta go to bed," I manage.

"What? We just got here. This song is great! Are you hearing this?" my dad says. He turns away. "I think we can get in through here. I saw a path here earlier on my run," my dad points to a gap in the fencing. His voice is soft. It echoes through my mind, which has swiftly gone hollow.

"Dad, I'm gonna pass out. I took Seroquel," I say.

I try to spit the words out before the inevitable exhaustion steals my ability to speak.

"You're not going to pass out. Geez!" he says, "Let's at least stay a few minutes. We will go back soon. Why didn't you tell me you were tired?"

I blackout.

I feel the steady pace of my father's stride and realize I am being carried like a child in my Free People tube-dress.

Cool.

The faint sound of Bon Jovi's voice softens and disappears.

"He sounds great, Kali. By the way, I didn't know that you fall asleep...like immediately," my dad says out of breath.

I try to answer but am unable; the familiar feeling of being pressed between a human-size waffle-maker consumes me. I've been Seroquel'd.

Dr. Morano Goes iRobot

"Just this way," the nurse says, as she leads us down the long hallway of Dr. Morano's office, "The doctor is trying something new. He will be seeing you remotely today."

"Huh? Like through a computer?" my mom asks.

"He will be on a flat screen, in real time of course," she says.

"What? Why?" my mom says.

"Just something new that he's trying out," she answers and motions toward the pair of chairs next to the exam table, "You can sit here. He will be with you shortly."

She walks over to the flat screen and turns it on. Dr. Morano walks into frame. His Hawaiian shirt is strikingly odd against the backdrop of what looks like his own home.

"Hey, there!" he says.

What the...

My mother starts laughing.

At the end of the cyber appointment, the nurse hands me a plastic bag full of Geodon and Topamax samples. I am instructed to stay on the Lamictal and the Seroquel as well as add in Geodon and Topamax. (See Appendix L.)

Dr. Morano M.D. (psychiatrist): June 07, 2007
Seroquel 100mg
Lamictal 200mg
Samples of Geodon
Samples of Topamax (started in May)

Prom: A Night to Forget

Prom night is far from elegant. The night starts off perfectly. I have on the black A-line dress I'd gotten at Saks. It's understated, and a throwback, but the black pumps spice it up a bit.

I got my makeup done and am sporting winged eyeliner. I even got my hair done. It is down with a poof up front like the Fifties.

Prom is boring, as expected, but it is a little cool to be invited to Prom as an underclassman. We leave the dance early to go back to Trey's and relax.

I change out of my prized dress, and into one of Trey's tees and some workout shorts. Just as I am beginning to relax, Blaise grabs my arm. I already started drinking, so I stumble as he pulls me up. Blaise is mad. He tightens his grip on my wrist.

I black out.

I wake up in a dark room. Blaise is there. He's standing over me. I'm sitting on the carpet leaning up against the bed frame. My head keeps bobbing forward like a doll as he shoves me.

"You told me you wouldn't drink," Blaise says under his breath, "Are you kidding me?" He kneels down next to me and grabs me by the shoulders. "Wake the FUCK UP Kali!"

He's shaking me.

I black out.

I go to lunch with Blaise the day after prom. A few different people alerted me that there had been some commotion in Ryan's room after Prom.

Ryan is Jarrod, the host's, younger brother. Ryan couldn't get into his room. And Blaise, reportedly, refused to open the door for him. Standing by the door to get in, Ryan and Jordan both heard some unsettling noises coming from inside. They realized it was me and became worried that Blaise was being rough with me. They tried to get Blaise to open the door so that they could check things out, and he wouldn't.

I am not sure if it is a good thing or a bad thing that I cannot remember a thing except for the few moments Blaise is shouting at me in the dark for drinking. I starred in a mini-drama on Prom night that I was not conscious enough to watch.

"People were scared last night," I tell Blaise.

"Ha! About what?" Blaise says.

"About you and how you treated me," I say.

"What are you talking about?" Blaise says. He sort of twitches his shoulder and looks at me humored. "I was so gone last night. I blacked out before I got to Jarrod's."

He doesn't acknowledge the comment, continuing to walk through the food court.

"People were afraid you were hurting me. You know you gave me this bruise?" I point to my right upper arm. Blaise grabs it.

"You give me bruises all the time too, punk," Blaise says.

He pushes into me, and I stumble out of my steady gait. I forget what I am trying to accomplish with this conversation.

My heart is racing, clouding my thoughts. I search for words but find nothing to say. I don't want to upset him, and I realize he will never acknowledge what he did because he doesn't care.

Are you still around? This is your choice, Kali.

I look down at my left wrist. There are three fingerprint bruises lined up in a crooked row, red/purple against my pale skin. My mind wanders back to the night before, as I trace the blue veins from the base of my wrist like rivers on a map. My wrist looks more delicate than usual. I never paid much attention until then.

"I'll get the bean and cheese burrito and a Coke," Blaise says. We were at the La Salsa counter. I forgot we were walking there. Blaise has an energetic, awkward way of moving. He bounces, but not nerdy, more athletic; think coke head meets jock.

He slides the plastic tray across the metal rails of the counter before swooping it up and walking toward the "Pick Up" side of the food counter.

"I'll just get the kids...never mind, actually. Do you have Diet Coke?" I ask.

Dr. Scott M.D. (GP): July 18, 2007
Medications: Synthroid, Lamictal, Geodon, Topamax
Chief Complaint: Sports Physical
S: Started new meds for psych "going well," per mom. Bipolar improved

Blaise's Guest House: Things Speed Up

Blaise's father lived in a mansion on Balboa Island, right on the water; boasting its own private dock, filled with perfectly groomed carpets and crystal-clear glass tables. There was a cliché Newport Coast family photo, embossed in a gold frame, glossy and perfectly placed over the fireplace. The shiny photograph captured Blaise, his younger sister Belle, his father, and his stepmother, Elisabeth, Liza, with a hard z.

Attached to the four-bedroom house was a guesthouse. The only entrance to it was up a flight of stairs outside, to the left of the main house. It had its own key and everything. This kind of guesthouse would usually be rented out. But, I wasn't living in a "usual" world.

Instead, Blaise's father gave Blaise the keys, hoping to cut down the incidents of Blaise waking Liza up when he came in late. Now, when Blaise came home at three a.m., messed up with his buddies, he would have a completely separate apartment to crash in: it was his "party house."

I hated that place. I still hate that place.

I open the door to Blaise's guesthouse; Elodie and Kayley follow me in, the only two takers for the late-night trip to the island.

Blaise is on the phone, pacing. His "gang" friend, Mike, is chopping up what I think is cocaine on the glass table in the kitchen. There is a pile about the size of my fist in the center of the table. He isn't working with it. He sectioned off a portion, hunched over the fine white powder. After every several dozen cuts with his credit card, he carefully scoots the powder back into a smaller pile. I soon learn what he is doing. A few minutes and some small talk later, Mike separates five distinct lines. They are about half the size of a pencil.

We'd all been drinking for hours. It was late summer and a perfect night.

Elodie's mascara is already running under her bottom lid. She is wearing some guy's sweatshirt.

Kayley looks just as tired, but each of them jumps off the leather sofa when called.

Kayley goes first. She sits on Mike's lap, confidently, takes one of the dollars lying on the table, rolls it into a tight tube and plugging one nostril, snorts the entire line.

Aw. So that's how it works.

Elodie is more reticent than Kayley. But Blaise helps her.

Leave it to my boyfriend to help you snort your first line of cocaine.

Elodie is a writer, very intelligent and a stable individual. She looks over at me with a look of near-Zen elation. I take a seat in the third chair around the glass table where the mound of white powder sits. I follow suit and carefully roll up the twenty-dollar bill Blaise pulls out of his money clip.

"Need help?" Blaise asks; his voice is different than usual, sweeter, like when I'd met him at water polo practice.

"Is this right?"

"Yeah, here. Just let me make it a little tighter."

I place it in his palm. He re-rolls the twenty, swiftly but perfectly. He smiles and hands it back to me. "You know how to do this?" Blaise asks.

"Nope. Not at all," I say.

"Here..." Blaise says.

He comes up beside me and takes me through a step-by-step instruction of how to correctly and elegantly snort coke.

"You can use the same nostril or switch. Just plug the one you're not using," Blaise says.

I watch his jaw grind back and forth. He has a sort of twitch about him.

"You excited?" Blaise asks.

He tickles my ribs and pulls me into him like a rag doll. He is high, but he's kind.

"Stop! Let me..." I say, being my usual stubborn self.

Blaise walks away, joking with Mike about something. I put the little rolled-up money-straw up my nose, plug one nostril and inhale. It's bitter. I stop midway down the line, out of breath, to take another inhale and retrace my steps to get all of the dust. It was like a game. And—

Whoa.

I'm numb.

"Wait, holy shit, dude. Your girl just—oh my god, bro," Mike says.

"Wait—"

Blaise bursts out laughing.

"Oh my God, Kali, did you just take the line that was separate from the others?" Blaise says.

"Yeah. Yeah," I say, feeling the effects of what I'd just done.

Blaise laughs so hard that he falls out of his chair.

"Well, this will be fun," Blaise says.

My eyes hyper-focus on Kayley and dart to Elodie, whose jaw is moving like Blaise's now.

"What-what-what did I do wrong?" I ask.

Whoa, I feel weird.

"Kali, you snorted like six lines just now. That was not a line. That was the supply we had for the night. It was the pile we were dividing," Mike says.

Uh oh.

"Am I gonna die?"

He laughs, "Nah, you're just a champ, my champ."

He continues to laugh with Mike who is choked up; he's laughing so hard.

I wake up the next morning and immediately call Tessa.

"Oh my God!" I shout into the phone.

"Kali, it's like eight a.m.," she sounds groggy. "Why are you up, crazy girl?"

"I've figured everything out. Instead of drinking, I'm just going to do coke. It's great! I'm not hung-over, and I remember, kind of..."

"Kali, did Blaise give you coke last night?"

"Yeah."

"Fucking Blaise...Please call me later today. You won't feel this great forever. Try to sleep. Love you. Oh and that's the worst idea I've ever heard like EVER. "

I don't know what she is referring to, I feel great! It is early! The clouds are going to fade, and the sun will be SHINING SOON! I LOVE LIFE!

A couple of hours later, I am devising ways to take my own life. I am actually planning it. I have been struggling with depression, but not this kind.

This kind ached to think, hurt to move, and the guilt was stifling. I had no way out, and I was a burden. In a haze, I searched for all the ways I could do this. I could think of nothing more. It was time. I had no reasons anymore. All of a sudden, my phones rings, it's Tessa. I watch ring, no emotionless, no sense of reason. She must have called thirteen times. I finally press the green button but don't put it up to my ear; I am too tired even to try.

"Kali! Don't do anything stupid. I'm on my way over."

"I'm done," I mumble.

"Fucking Blaise, I'll be there soon, stay in bed, turn on SpongeBob if you're in Kayla's room...Please. Love you bye."

Tessa stayed with me all day and night. I never left my room. My mother thought I had the flu. Tessa corrects me when I tell her I want to die.

"Yeah I've totally felt that sick before, it's the worst, and I hear it's going around," Tessa adds. And I don't have the strength to restate what I am trying to say.

"Blaise is an asshole, Kali. NEVER do coke again. You are different. He should have known," Tessa says before she leaves.

It Didn't Hurt Me

Going into Junior Year of high school, I end up at the guesthouse for the second time. The repercussions of this night lasted longer than the daylong suicidal depression of the first. The last thing I remember is being carried up the stairs to the door.

"Ssshh!" Blaise says as I wake up at the top of the staircase to the guesthouse. I lift my head to see the bay: Newport Bay. It's navy blue in the moonlight, not black. It must be early morning.

Things go black.

Opening my eyes, I find myself inside. I can barely see Blaise, but I can tell it's him. He is in the bedroom. I must be on the couch.

Please don't try anything.

I try to lift my head up to look around. But this time my body denies my request.

I blackout.

I wake up to Blaise, yelling, playfully, but yelling all the same. He's approaching me. I am sprawled across the sofa.

What happened to the quiet thing? He must have done coke.

"Get the fuck up! Or I'll pour this on you..." Blaise says.

He's holding what looks like a glass of water over me. I try to get my eyes to focus and find that he's naked. Things start swimming again and then black.

I blackout.

About a week earlier, I had a discussion with Tessa at school.

We are walking through the quad at Break when I feel the urge to confess her something I'd been obsessing over.

"I want to wait for marriage. It makes it something to look forward to," I say.

"Really? Wow, Dude. That's rad," Tessa says, "I like having sex with Liam. But if he weren't around, I'd probably wait too."

And now, here I am, having no recollection of that supposedly sacred encounter. I don't remember how I got home or really anything past Blaise's blurry figure and my spotty memory of shouting at him from the bedroom to stop. He must have carried me into the bedroom. There's no way I could have walked.

It's almost 3 p.m., and I've been in the bathroom for hours. I want to throw up my insides and cry all at the same time. I went to take a shower and all at once, it hit me. I feel used up for good: I can't get clean.

I ended up taking a few showers, trying to erase the dirt left over. I can't get clean. It is all over for me now. I'm used up. I'm spending my afternoon in the bathtub. No music. Silence. Disgust.

Tessa stops by later in the evening after I hadn't responded to any texts or calls. She's irritated by it and is studying her cell phone on my bed. Her attitude makes me feel sick. I hadn't meant to leave her the night before. I don't remember.

"Blaise had sex with me when I was passed out," I word vomit to Tessa. "What THE FUCK Kali! Did you lose it? He fucked you while you were passed out? And it was your FIRST TIME?" Tessa shouts nearly throwing down her phone. She gets off the bed and begins to pace. By her breathing, I can tell she is livid, but I feel nothing. I've already become hardened to the entire ordeal.

"I'm going to fucking kill him. Can I please tell Liam so Liam can fuck him up? Please," Tessa begs.

At school the next day, I am already being asked about it.

What do you know? Word got around. Thanks to my stellar boyfriend, Blaise. He had bragged to his friends who talked among each other enough for it to get all the way around to my friends. At least, I can tell my shocked friends that, contrary to popular belief: "it totally didn't hurt at all."

I cannot remember a thing about that night, except for the staircase, the blurry of Blaise yelling at me, and that pitiful struggle on the bed, which I obviously lost, but wasn't awake to notice.

The incessant scrubbing the next morning though did, in fact, hurt.

My mind is usually my worst enemy, but not in this case. It placed a black, rectangular, censor-box on top of that night until now. Thankfully, I never had to pull up that night before. I decided that it didn't happen and refused to think of it again. My journal entries tell a different story. Although they don't ever say specifics, I am guilty of always keeping one eye open, the feeling of utter devastation is more than prevalent in the entries following. My writing takes an immediate turn into oblivion, and I struggled to figure out why.

An Enlightening Urgent Care Visit

At an Urgent Care facility in Newport Coast, the doctor I've seen since I was a toddler mentions the list of medications I am on as "a cocktail." Nodding in agreement, I want to add to her statement, but something is up. The words I want to speak are unattainable.

Words are tools for me. I spend a lot of time trying to explain how I feel, hoping to transfer those feelings to the person in which I am conversing.

Words allow me to be understood; at least, I believe, they allow for that, somewhat. Words are everything to me. Recently, though, I've lost the toolbox.

The wax-like paper on the table crinkles under me as I swing my leg over the other, shifting positions, awkwardly unable to spit it out. The dictionary pages I envision as I prepare to speak seem to have the words blanked out. As I zoom in to grab one to use, they vaporize just out of reach. I can see the black letters from afar, but as I try to focus, the words vanish.

"Wow," I say, opening my mouth to speak, and finding no words, Again.

"Yes?" Dr. Roberts says.

"I can't find the words..." I say.

"Does that happen a lot?" she asks.

"Yes..."

The statement throws me into an introspective discovery state where I find that:

"Yes! It's happened for months, now that I think about it. I can't seem to remember any words."

"Hmm, are you still taking the Topamax?" Dr. Roberts asks.

Topamax is linked to this concept that I had no idea was a symptom of anything, other than my own, seemingly out of nowhere, decline in intelligence..

This is not my fault. The drug is making me forget things!

Within days of being off of Topamax, I feel like my brain has returned. I am on top of my game again in conversations with people and there is an overall ease in which I communicate. The floodgates to my mind have opened and I can finally speak what's on my mind. (See Appendix Q.)

Repercussions: The Leather Journal

August 06 2007

Wow, it's been a hard few weeks. I'm lost, and I know it, but I can't seem to find myself. I've been keeping myself busy doing stupid, meaningless tasks to waste time. It worked for a while, but for some reason, right now I feel as if I am continuously losing time and losing sight of my dreams. I'm scared to death of being in a relationship, and yesterday I had a mental breakdown and literally jumped out of Blaise's car to get away from him. I completely freaked out about having a relationship and didn't want to see him. I went to dance class but could hardly pull myself together. XO Kali Rae

August 07, 2007

I saw Sandy, my counselor, yesterday, like every Monday and as hard as I tried not to, I broke down in her office. She figured me out. She says I keep everyone at arm's distance, and that I'm truly very lonely and that's why I feel like I'm losing time and that's why I'm so afraid to say goodbye to anyone. Basically, I've never let anyone in. I feel like I'm losing and have already lost everyone. I'm alone. I'm scared of losing people I've never really had. I need to take my fucking pills. I've always felt like I don't need anyone, ever. I can do fine without anyone. I'm fine alone. I don't need anyone. Why do they need me? Am I back to square 1??

Later...
How come every time I leave Blaise I feel like I've done something wrong? It's like an overwhelming feeling of regret. Why? I don't understand myself. Every day I am regretting something, and if I'm not regretting hanging with Blaise, I'm regretting things I did drunk the night before.

When I'm drunk, I don't regret things. Everything is so much better when I'm drunk. Why is that? Why does drinking make me like him more and make me feel like I'm on top of the world? I forget about all the things that I'm struggling with. I forget the feelings of worthlessness and loss. Most of the time I don't even know what it is that I'm losing. I mostly feel that I'm losing time and opportunities and people. I can't stand to recognize the past; it upsets me too much...lost opportunities, memories I'll never get back. I have an overwhelming sense of not fulfilling what I'm supposed to be fulfilling. I will never get these moments back. What is it that I'm losing? I'm sick and tired of feeling like this. What have I lost? What memory is haunting me? Why can't I care about anyone?? Why don't I care about anything? What is wrong with me? HELP ME!! Why am I so alone...why do I force myself to be alone? Why am I so scared of being hurt?

Sandy says that if I continue to keep people at arm's distance, I will continue to feel this way, and when I remember memories I've shared with people there will only be an empty space and pain. That's what I have right now, empty space and pain. Sandy also tells me that no one can ever take away the memories. The memories are not lost and time isn't lost. I am sinking. Why does the past hurt so much? What have I lost? It feels like everything. I can't say goodbye. I just can't. I can't say goodbye. I need to find myself. XO Kali Rae

August 08, 2007

I was doing alright today...I guess. Or at least, I thought I was. I just drove Kendall home, and when I was almost to my house I found myself saying, "I want to kill myself, " and I couldn't stop saying this in a very monotone, emotionless voice. (See Appendix J.) It was if I was possessed or something. But what do I really have to live for? FUCK IT. Why am I so unhappy? Why am I such a NUT? I actually thought about what would happen if I ran my car off the road.

 I just ate so much my stomach is going to burst, and I feel HORRIBLE. I want someone so bad, but I push everyone away. How am I ever going to find comfort? A few hours ago I was bouncing off the walls happy, but that only lasted a few hours. That's how I feel. Why did I say those things in the car? Is it true? Do I really want to die? Do I give up? No! I can't give up! I will make it through! I am not a wimp! I will never give up. I will never quit. That is a promise. Why do I do this to myself? My body hurts...it's done with me. It hates me. I wish I was thin. I wish I was normal. I, Kali Rae Wheeler, solemnly swear, that I will NEVER give up.

 Why does it feel like I've lost everyone and everything? And why do I like it so much when members of my family go on vacation. Why don't I miss them and want them to come back? Why don't I love anyone? How can I love someone else when I don't even love myself? I don't know what I feel or think. I don't even know what I enjoy. I don't even know myself...at all. I scare myself. I'm scared of what I could do to myself. I hope I don't get tattoos or piercings. I want to die, I think. There. I got it out. Goodnight. I am SO LOST. I don't need anyone. I'll be fine alone. My stomach is hurting so bad I can't cry. Please body let me cry! I've lost something I can't replace.

Later...
 By the way, I'm really happy right now because I took double the Lamictal I was supposed to...definitely in the manic stage. I was severely depressed for the last week. Also, just wanted to add, it didn't hurt that bad my first time, maybe cause I was drunk. I don't remember. I was blacked out. I can't believe Blaise graduated! I have

dated him since March, so it's legit, that's like five months. Whoa!
XO Kali Rae

August 13, 2007

I want to die. XO Kali Rae

August 15, 2007

Why do I always feel like I've done something I regret? I didn't do anything. Is it something I said? Why do I always feel this way? I can't stand to live like this. I didn't drink today or yesterday. But today I took caffeine pills and drank a double Rockstar.

Lately, I've been extra thinking about doing coke. I'm just scared of how depressed I'd be after. Why do I feel like this? I am so uncomfortable in my own skin that it's kind of scary. Like I don't get why I'm always regretting something. I'm getting back on track. I know I am. Like I'm getting back to normal eating habits. I'll probably take more caffeine pills tomorrow. I wish I felt better about everything. The caffeine pills curb my appetite. I wish that losing weight was an instant fix...,but it's not.

It's late now, and I can't sleep. I keep pretending I feel okay, but I don't; I'm confused. My stomach hurts, and I don't know what to think about anything. I give up on trying to figure myself out.

I can't stand all these medications that don't fucking work. I don't even know what part of what I feel is actually me and what is the meds. Help Me. I can't do this anymore. I can't even tell if I'm happy or sad. XO Kali Rae (See Appendices F, J.)

August 16, 2007

Worst migraine ever, probably because I haven't eaten in two days. I can't figure out what's wrong with me. I am so bipolar. I can't sleep...of course! I really want to get my period. I'm sketching out even though he told me he wore a condom that night. Please let me get my period next week. Please. XO Kali Rae

Part IV:
Junior Year

Dr. Fiaschetti's Encyclopedia of Medications

My mother, Dr. Scott and Sandy are worried about Dr. Morano's prescribing tendencies. On top of everything else, Dr. Morano doesn't even have a proper office anymore. Sandy comes to the rescue. She recommends I go to see her friend, Dr. Fiaschetti, who can at least monitor what Dr. Morano is prescribing. What we don't know is that Dr. Fiaschetti is particularly good at the musical prescriptions game.

Dr. Fiaschetti has a gigantic canvas bound, book: probably two full-size Webster Dictionaries thick. It's her weapon. She has a beautiful office on the beach past Laguna.

Every appointment follows the same pattern; she receives my comments on the most recent drug, she has tried me on, writes notes on her legal pad about the side, walks across her office to flip through the book. She runs her finger along the pages, stops, announces an idea and then turns to a different page, does the same thing, and finally announces her conclusion: a new mixture of drugs.

I had been taking the samples of Geodon on top of Seroquel and Lamictal up until my first appointment with Fiaschetti in September of my Junior year. That first appointment, after going through each of the medications I had already tried and denied noting the adverse reactions, increases Lamictal to 125mg. Per her notes, when I increased the Lamictal, I "couldn't get out of bed."

The next visit, even after transcribing in her records that Dr. Morano took me off of Topamax "due to dizziness and word-finding issues" Dr. Fiaschetti reinstates the Topamax for headaches. Soon after, she increases it to 150mg.

Dr. Fiaschetti M.D. (psychiatrist): Before September 19, 2007
Prozac— "went psycho," shaking, singing in public, jumping around
Wellbutrin—crabby
Seroquel—slept, but felt like a "zombie."
Geodon—worked ok during the summer but in early classes at school you saw triple. Made you hyper for the 1st three hours after you took it and then groggy all the next day, didn't help.
Abilify—tired, migraines
Lamictal—back and forth 50, 75, 100
Lyrica—manic
Topamax—made you dizzy, and made it hard to remember words when you thought of them
Effexor—brain shivers

Dr. Fiaschetti M.D. (psychiatrist): September 19, 2007
Lamictal 75mg up to 125mg

Dr. Scott M.D. (GP): October 8, 2007
Medications: Synthroid, Lamictal
S: headaches, fatigue, pale skin
O: denies depression, "hanging in there," chills, feet numb
All symptoms began a month ago. (See Appendices F, J.)
Dx: acute sinusitis, fatigue, possible chronic fatigue syndrome vs. recovering from mononucleosis
A/P: CT scan of sinuses, CT scan of head
Rx Claritin, and amoxicillin

Dr. Fiaschetti M.D. (psychiatrist): October 17, 2007
Topamax 100mg added for a headache—later increased to 150mg

An Internship in the Hills

By Junior year, I am itching to start a life outside of the bubble that is my hometown.

My mom's friend, Marlene is a reporter who spends most of her time traveling around the world being styled by the best in the business. I somehow manage to convince her to let me plead my case and bring her my resume in the hopes that maybe she knows someone and will somehow be inspired by our discussion to hook me up. I spent all last weekend in Los Angeles dropping my resume of at all the major fashion houses. But, I was eager to start making things happen for myself. I make sure I look extra fashionable, even wearing a scarf, before making the short walk up the street to meet Marlene, resume in hand.

Within minutes she is calling her stylist, Marcus, to tell him I am coming up the next weekend. Flash forward another week, and I'm barging into his very private studio one Sunday afternoon, unknowingly, of course. I come to find out, at that moment, that these were store-front-looking places, but they weren't stores. Rather, officers, privates ones.

I open the door to the Hollywood studio and step over the doggy fence set up to keep on of the other designer's teacup Chihuahuas from running onto the crazy streets of Hollywood. Guessing the guy with the confused look on his face is Marcus, I blurt out, "Hi! I'm Kali!"

"Hiiii, how are you?"

He totally doesn't know who I am.

"Hi! I'm Kali's mom." My mom interrupts.

I turn around to find my mother standing outside of the studio, just hanging in the door frame. In or out mom, make your decision.

"Hi, Mom! Come on in. I'll show you guys around," Marcus says. Awkward.

Long story short, I got the job! And it was magical. I felt that I had discovered a whole new world that only I could break into because I had the guts to walk into a million fashion houses with a resume. The process spits me out in the perfect spot: hand-gluing rhinestones to the back of the tights of an American Idol performer, learning the actual culture of cross-dressing, by being exposed to Marcus and his fabulously-kind fiancé, Hunter.

Hunter always made me feel not only welcome but also necessary. He made me feel like I was integral to the group. He introduced me to everyone who entered the studio, including all of the artist's managers and spent most of the day sewing or putting together new pieces, chatting with me about this and that and showing me everything from how to sew on a button properly to how to organize a celebrity's closet properly.

I got to see the fabric room and learn about how he came up in the industry.

The studio space doubled as a mini-shop and event space. Aside from the main studio, there is a mirrored room for hair and makeup, storage room, an additional upstairs for fabric storage space, and a large room for the actual photo shoots. This area was used for the weekly Yoga class come Sunday. The patio shared a wall with a popular club in LA at the time, one that had gained attention on a hit television show.

One afternoon in the shop Marcus had one of his typical Marcus Morello moments. Marcus looks over at me, a devious look in his eyes, or was it envy? He always seemed to covet my body. Hunter's helping me put together a piece for a new pop artist. Marcus stops what he's doing.

"I want to look like Kali. She's so skinny and flat-chested." He rounds his shoulders, putting his hands on his hips. "And she's all hunch-y and model-y." He juts his elbows out and forward, pursing his lips and sucking in his cheeks.

"Marcus! You can't say that to her!" Hunter shouts, knowing like I did, that Marcus means well. "You're beautiful Honey; you have a flawless chest."

"That's not what I meant! She's gorgeous! I was saying like she's like..." Marcus hunches his back into a c-shape, throwing his shoulders dramatically forward, sucking in his stomach and popping his front knee. He stares off inquisitively. He then tries to recreate the Blue-Steel look. I'm laughing hard by this point. It was an eye-opening internship.

I serve as the resident mannequin, aside from my assistant duties. Whenever Marcus needs something fitted for an artist, I am there.

"Arms up!" Marcus says.

I remove my James Perse cotton long sleeve and let it drop to the floor of the studio. Marcus is already pulling the top over my head. "Turn around Hun," he says. Marcus carefully brings his fingers underneath the material to keep the pins from piercing me as he slides it onto my chest. "Excuse me!" he shouts animated; his eyes widen in jest as he maneuvers the top past my chest. I laugh.

In the name of fashion!

This is our routine, and I trust Marcus explicitly. I have no reason no to; he's one of my favorite people ever.

At times, I feel uncomfortable, but it is while staring at the nude paintings of male genitalia lining the walls alongside designs for men's strap ons. I saw it all in Marcus's studio. Nothing fazed me. There were dozens of man on man genital portraits complete with red paint coming out of male parts. I didn't like that last part.

I kept my eyes down while working. The paintings line the space, on a shelf about halfway up the high ceilings of the posh studio space. I kept my eyes down most of the time. I was too curious not to look up.

Dr. Scott M.D. (GP): December 18, 2007
Add: Call w/Mom
Will lower Lamictal
Morano to consider changing Topamax

More Diagnosis, Fewer Answers

September of my Junior year I feel like I have been run over by a truck. Everything is a task. The notes from an appointment with Dr. Scott further illustrate this.

I went in to see him for a simple sinus infection. But, it was at that appointment that Dr. Scott explained to me that the length and intensity of the mononucleosis made it almost inevitable that I get chronic fatigue syndrome. He introduced to me the idea that I may not just be recovering from mononucleosis, but that I may have a new illness. I denied all feelings that he could be right. There was no way that I would have to endure this level of shittiness my entire life. I simply wouldn't be able to handle it.

A month later, in December, Dr. Scott notes that I should have Morano "consider changing out Topamax (for multiple reasons, including difficulty finding words and dizziness) and to lower the Lamictal." In March of 2008, Dr. Morano takes me off of Lamictal. But, by this time, I am more apathetic than ever. I am giving up.

Cruel Humor and Witnessing Terror in a Bystander

It was a slow night at Trey's. His parents' home often served as home base for the weekend nights' escapades.

His parents were never around. They were older and stayed in their rooms, behind closed doors, if they were home. The front part of the house, which included the living room, dining room, and kitchen, was closed off from the back bedrooms. Although it wasn't a mansion, it was the perfect party house. Trey had people over every Friday and Saturday.

People got drunk at Trey's, left to go to a party for the night, and would return here, wasted, to drink more until the evening turned back into day, and do it all over again.

Trey's shiny new BMW showcases itself in all of its new-car glory. There is even a red bow tied around it, just like those commercials that play during Christmastime to remind us Californians that, no, you will not have a white Christmas. There won't be snow sifted carefully onto the hood of your shiny black Benz Christmas morning.

The car had been gifted to Trey that afternoon. Having had his license taken away, due to a DUI last summer, Trey had no license to drive it yet. It was his graduation present for being accepted into the University of Arizona, Trey told us.

A handful of us are hanging around the brushed-wood table tonight. Each of us carrying moderately filled glasses of the alcohol of our choice. I'm sipping a ginger ale drink that Trey spent a decent amount of time making. I feel sophisticated gripping the clear, crystal glass. Olivia is next to me. She isn't drinking at all. I knew she wouldn't be. Jessalyn is sitting across the table from me next to Reed. I liked Reed's company. He didn't ever say much, but his presence made me relax a little.

Olivia is one of my first friends from a different school than my elementary school. She has an older sister in Isaak's grade and a couple of younger brothers. Olivia is the ultimate diva but in an entirely elegant, quasi Janis Joplin way. She always has the trendiest clothes and tries out the new styles first. Olivia is the friend I go to for wild experiences, things that I like to do. At one point we decided to climb onto the roof of her house naked and tan our butts. It went well until the gardeners showed up and we had no escape plan or anything to throw over us.

Her cousin, Jessalyn, lived on the same street as her. They were on again off again frenemies, but they are family, so no one knows what's up with that. Jessalyn is much more traditional: Sperry's shoes, Lacoste shirt, Paper Denim Jeans. A classic, relaxed Newport housewife look. Jess is much quieter from an outside perspective, but super loud when you knew her. Jess is the kind of girl who comes out of nowhere with an on point but a pretty rude comment about another girl. We didn't always get along because of this. Jessalyn, at one point, told our group of girls:

"Kali's just too cool."

To which Olivia inquired, "Like she just thinks she's too cool? Or…"

"No, she's just too cool," Jess answered.

This meaningless conversation plays ceaselessly back to me whenever I try to decipher why the heck Jess is acting frosty.

Trey's best friend Reed is the guy who always seems to be watching out for me. He is off limits for me, though, a self-imposed rule. I am not sure why, except that he doesn't have girlfriends. He doesn't have much of anything that isn't a surfboard, surf videos or skater tees. But he is fascinating to me. I keep a sweater he lent me for months. He gave it to me after a significantly stressful night, and it made me feel safe. I wish I still had it: the teal, red and white thick stripes, and its light cotton blend felt like a barrier: an eraser, a new start.

Olivia reportedly spent Christmas break super tired, hungry and cranky. Her symptoms began after she openly slept with one of the boys at our school, multiple times, unprotected.

After overhearing Olivia describe her symptoms to me on the phone, my mother, who I'd been Christmas-decorating with, got on the phone with Olivia to clarify why she felt sick and to tell her what she needed to do about it.

"Go to the doctor." My mom nods her head and continues. "Right. Yes. Yes. Olivia, you are pregnant."

Olivia's pregnancy had only become a drama when the father of the baby, Wyatt, denied everything, even those drunken nights that we'd all seen. Wyatt denied all of the events.

Wyatt and Olivia were not secretive at all about what they were doing. At one point, they had sex in a bush next door to a house where he was throwing a party—his friends even shouted to him in their drunken stupor.

"Wyatt! Where are the cups?" They laughed harder when Wyatt answered out of breath.

Wyatt was now, not only refusing to acknowledge Olivia but also refusing to help pay for the abortion. He wouldn't claim any responsibility and now refused to answer Olivia's calls, having heard the news of her alleged pregnancy through the grapevine. The guy was found to be a complete an utter asshole. Wyatt was the kind of asshole that even assholes look down upon.

It was enough time for Newport to accept Olivia's pregnancy or at least the Newport Coast side of the Bay. Tessa had apparently been one of the first to hear about Olivia's pregnancy via Olivia (we were all best friends), but Tessa allegedly told some people at Newport Beach High School–Tessa was transferred to Beach after a security guard searched her car and found marijuana. They were in result now enemies.

The news had spread around the city like wildfire, and there were rumors that Olivia was taking a bat to her stomach. As you see, our town has a lot of time on their hands.

Olivia consciously decided, early on, that she was going to have the baby. And since that decision, Olivia had shifted into a new person. Her demeanor changed dramatically with the pregnancy.

Olivia has done a one-eighty, from dramatic teen to mature, fully grown-up measured adult. Olivia was sure of her decision, and people didn't bring it up. When she decided to come out on the weekends for an hour or so, baby bump and all, no one brought it up. There was no need.

It was Olivia's pregnancy, as well as the general laid-back mood of the place, that set an interesting tone for the night. It would be a calm evening.

We'd even left the front doors open, letting the salty breeze of the summer night into the living room.

As soon as we get comfortable with our newly sophisticated social hour, a car comes to a quick stop in front of the house. A couple of loud voices pierce the darkness of the quiet neighborhood.

Shit.

I look over at Olivia.

Shit.

I recognize Blaise's voice right before he bursts through the door. Olivia rolls her eyes. "Great," she says, unamused.

Blaise is in college now, albeit the local university, but still! He was supposed to be out of my hair.

Trey stands up to block Blaise and Erol from getting through the doorframe. "Whoa, guys," says Trey. He's holding Blaise and Erol back with his arm, but it won't hold. The two boys burst through, gang headbands, black tees, Rolexes and white Converse. This outfit was the Lord's gang uniform, no joke.

Erol is Blaise's new best friend. He was a stark contrast to the other water polo boys that star water polo player Blaise usually hung around. Erol is a well-known member of the local gang. And, it looks like Blaise is now a member too.

I silently chuckle at the fact that Blaise thinks he's a member. They are clearly using him. Blaise is cool, in a star athlete, funny guy way, not as a gang member. But he was great at being a misnomer.

Blaise's eyes are wild as he charges over to me. He looks stupid, but it doesn't make him less terrifying. He pulls my chair out from under the table, throwing me off with it.

"Yo. Give me your seat," Blaise says and laughs, watching me topple to the ground. He sits down in the empty chair next to me. I iron my denim skirt back down with my hands and get off the ground to sit at the table again.

No fear. Act strong. He was your boyfriend. It's 'just Blaise.

His jaw is clenching, grinding side-to-side.

He's high. Fuck.

"What's up, Olivia? Aren't you supposed to be at the abortion clinic?" Blaise asks Olivia, leaning toward her, sitting in a power position like usual, legs spread.

Trey, Jessalyn, and Reed sit quietly in disbelief. The broken environment is tangible.

"Um, that would be dumb, because I am not getting an abortion Blaise," says Olivia.

Jessalyn, seated next to Reed on the opposite side of the table, slides her seat out. "I'm leaving. Anyone need a ride?"

Olivia looks over at Erol and then me and shakes her head. "I'll come back later tonight with Reed," Olivia says.

I didn't realize what Olivia was doing until months later.

Avoiding my direction, Jessalyn responds, "Whatever, Olivia," and then, "Thanks, Trey," as she heads for the door.

"Wait, so what happened, Olivia?" Blaise asks.

Why is he here?

"Blaise, shut up," I say between clenched teeth. It's almost snake-like. I am so angry, I'm hot. If I had fangs, I would have torn him to shreds.

"Kali, let's have a fucking chat. How about that?" Blaise says.

I didn't mean to say that out loud. It just came out of me in anger, and now I am screwed.

His eyes are the most vacant I've ever seen them. He grabs my left arm, picking me up with a jolt. My leg gets smashed between the table and the chair. The chair falls over toward him.

I realize I'm more intoxicated than I thought or planned. I didn't stand up since arriving.

The moment slows down as I catch Reed staring at Blaise with a look I'd never seen before. Then I turn my head the other way and realize that almost everyone, including Trey, has vacated the house.

The emptiness is stifling.

I'm in trouble.

I look back at the table again and see Olivia seated in the same place she was posted up all night. Erol is standing by the front door that is still left ajar. Reed is on the front porch outside now, pacing. He seems to be in a predicament.

"Blaise, don't be stupid," Olivia says nonchalantly while staring down at her phone.

Erol looks worried, and within a split second, I know that I am a victim. My job is to worry about my safety. I see it in their eyes. I am alone in this. No one else knows what to do to pacify Blaise.

Blaise shoves me toward the hallway and into a bedroom I didn't know existed. The doors to the hall are usually shut to keep the noise from getting to Trey's parent's room at the back of the house.

Blaise flicks on the light and slams the wicker double doors of the small room shut. He turns around for an instant before turning back around to make sure the doors lock from the inside.

"You drink? You drink, little girl?" Blaise says.

He taunts me over and over again. "You think that was smart Kali?"

Then he shoves me with such force I fall to the carpet next to the bed. He's stronger than I expected. His eyes aren't focusing. I can feel his anger. It's seeping out of him.

Who was he mad at?

"You told me you wouldn't drink," Blaise says.

"How could you say that to Olivia? How could you?" I say meekly.

I can't ever hold my tongue at the right times.

"Don't fucking look at me like that," Blaise responds and kicks the doors, so they rumble the walls. It sounds like thunder. I'm terrified. I know Blaise's dad beats him up, but Blaise is supposed to be different.

I try to stand up, and he shoves me back down to the carpet. I hoist myself up, leaning on my elbow.

"Oh! You want to get up? You want to get up? Yeah right. You can't stand up. You're too drunk." He walks toward me.

He shoves my arm this time, the one I'd been leaning into, and my body crashes into the carpet ill equip to handle his blows. My head hits the ground with a thud.

I was not ready for that.

"You're too drunk, Kali. You told me you wouldn't drink. What are you doing?" He answers himself as he fidgets: "You're being fucking stupid is what you're doing."

He laughs and punches the white door so hard that it rattles on the hinges once more. I hoist myself up to seated as he studies the rattling door.

He senses it and turns around.

"Get. The. Fuck. Down Kali."

He stomps back over to me, and I'm afraid he'll run right over me before he shoves me with both hands. It feels like being hit by two metal rods on in each shoulder. The blow is so forceful that I watch his body retract from it as I fall once more onto the beige carpet of this seemingly perfect bedroom.

I didn't even know this room existed before ten minutes ago.

Does anyone know this place exists? Does anyone know I'm in here?

The growing intensity of the secluded room and the completely fucked-out-of-his-mind condition Blaise is in causes adrenaline to surge through my intoxicated veins. My body sees real trouble.

I am suddenly very sober.

I need to get out of here.

I hear Erol's voice, confidently, but concerned, through the wicker part of the door. "Yo, Blaise! Man, open the door. I gotta tell you something," Erol says.

Thank God for these wicker panels. They can hear me.

"I have to go home. Please let me out," I say, half wishing Blaise won't hear me so that I wouldn't get hurt.

Blaise snaps his gaze back to me from the door.

"You've got to be fucking kidding me, Kali." Kneeling down, he gets right into my face. "You are too drunk to go home," Blaise says.

He smashes his palm into my chest, and I'm laid out again. This time I'll stay down. "And I'm going to teach you what drinking does to you because you look like a fucking idiot." He continues.

The world shakes or shivers, and I'm not sure if it's due to the hit or the alcohol.

"Yo, Blaise, serious, we've got to go!" Erol says with more intensity. "Open the fucking door, man."

"One second!" Blaise shouts back.

"No dude. Now!" Erol shouts.

Erol is angry. I hear Olivia talking to him.

"Go outside, Olivia. Blaise, dude, I'm going to kick this door open, and you're going to pay for it. Let's leave!" Erol shouts through the door.

Blaise is holding the shaking doors closed. His eyes scan my face and then my body. "You look so stupid right now. You can't even help yourself."

Blaise rips the blouse off of the shoulder I am leaning into and pushes me back onto my back. He stands up straight, straddling me, standing above me like some sick criminal. I don't look up, keeping my eyes in an empty gaze at the wicker doors I'm hoping will burst open shortly.

"Take off your skirt," Blaise says.

I don't move.

"I'm not kidding. I'll fucking kill you, dude."

I don't even think he can see me anymore. The doors of the room burst open, smacking the walls behind them. I cover my chest instinctively as Erol pulls Blaise up by the shirt collar.

"Let's. Fucking. Go." Erol says to Blaise and then looks down at me.

Erol's eyes soften and then look horrified before they harden up once more.

"Let's go...Now, Blaise!" Erol says again, looking away.

I see Olivia for a moment. She's right outside of the double doors.

"Olivia, why the fuck are you still here?" Blaise shouts as he passes her. "Go get your God damn abortion done."

Erol shoves Blaise toward the front door. "If you talk like that to her again, Bro, we aren't cool," Erol says.

I am too afraid to say a word. I don't want to turn the situation back to the red zone. My goal, along with everyone else's here, is to keep Blaise focused on leaving Trey's house.

I can hear Reed now from the kitchen.

"Just leave, bro. Nobody wants you here. I'll call the cops." Reed warns.

Blaise doesn't respond. He struggles loose from Erol's grip. Erol throws an arm up to protect Olivia, blocking her from harm. Erol stares Blaise down the entire way out of the house.

The front door slams shaking the wicker doors again: a now bone-chilling sound.

He Almost Drove Me Home

It is dark in here: dark and cramped. A streetlight reveals a tiny area of the vehicle's interior. I can't see anything. I feel the scratchy floor mats against my neck and back. I will be developing an ugly bruise.

My right leg stuck under the weight of Blaise, I am crammed into the crease of the door. My knee is scratching against the speaker embedded in the door itself.

"Where are we? Where's my phone? Stop! Where's my phone?" I yell.

It is morning-blue outside, not the black I remembered it being last night at Trey's. Then I see it.

Blaise's black tee bounces past Olivia and then Reed. He wriggles free of Erol's grasp, tries to turn around, gives up and stumbles out the door. I watch the moment when Erol sees me on the ground, and his gaze softens. I remember Jessalyn leaving and Olivia staying without any word about it.

I see Reed pacing outside.

Exhale.

It was over.

I pull my blouse onto my shoulder and throw my hair into a messy bun.

I black out.

Why was I with Blaise again?

I thought we had gotten rid of him! I figured I was safe! What about Reed? Olivia? Erol even? Where had the hours gone?

"Wait!" I shout. I sound desperate as my voice cracks.

I try to move out from underneath him, but he presses down hard. "Ow! Blaise, stop! I need to call Tessa. Wait! I'm supposed to be sleeping at Tessa's!"

"Tessa doesn't care. Don't call her. DON'T call her," he says and then repeats in a more stern fashion. He stops the pressure into me and increases the pressure he has on my wrists.

It begins again.

"Shut up Kali. Your phone is at Trey's. You were too drunk. You left it there." Blaise then shouts, "Stop moving!"

"Stop! Where is my phone? Where is my phone?" I cry out, pleading with him to stop.

I shift out from under him without warning and quickly move my knee in front of my body in a last-ditch show of strength.

It works!

On task, he slips out.

"That fucking hurt!" Blaise slams his hands on my legs.

I feel devious enjoying his pain. But I lose pride quickly. He grabs my leg harder and thrusts it open, increasing the pressure of his knee into the top of my thigh exponentially.

"Stop! You're hurting me!" I yell.

"Stop moving!" he says, leaning more weight onto my pinned knee. It is so painful that it burns. He is flattening my muscle with his bone.

Silence.

I go numb. My eyes glass over.

"Kali, why the fuck did you drink? I had to carry you out. Everyone left you. I had to take your car," Blaise says. My blood runs cold as the draining feeling of embarrassed presses in on me hard. I am especially embarrassed because I planned to stay at Tessa's with Olivia and Kendall. Blaise kept me from ruining their night. I look away from him, and suddenly, I realize that we are in my car. The back seat is folded down; I didn't recognize it.

I flinch as much as I can, which is only about an inch, hoping to seal myself off from him. I try to move my arms, but I am pinned beneath him.

"Stop! Please! Get off me!" I shout. My heart is finally racing back to life.

Blaise grunts and finishes.

I am disgusted. All I want to do is take a shower and wash myself from the inside out, to scrub my bones clean. Blaise laughs, as he peels off his shirt, wiping himself down before throwing it over to me.

I sit up. The world spins so quickly, I almost puke. I regain balance (sitting at least), but my head swings on my neck like a broken doll.

"Where the fuck is my phone?" I hiss, almost puking for the second time.

"I have it."

He pulls it out of his back pocket and presents it to me like it's a gift.

I turn on my phone and see seventeen missed calls; a majority of them are from the girls at Trey's, and several are from my parents. I scroll down to earlier in the night, and a text from my brother sends reverberating shock waves through me. The thought of my brother checking on me about what had just happened throws me into an overhaul of sickening emotions. It is such a polar opposite feeling that I have to hold myself back from vomiting. I am undeserving of my brother's love.

The hope I had mustered drains from my body as the phone freezes; a text to Tessa, stuck in the Outbox. The little round icon spins, and the phone shut off: battery dead.

I feel cold from head to foot for a moment before the hot, feverish, flu feeling overwhelms me again. My entire body aches, my head feels bashed in. I look out the window, and I recognize the house to the right. I glance to the left and recognize that house as well. Disbelief washes over me. But, I am too tired to question the place I find myself.

"I'll take you home in the morning," Blaise says from the front seat. He'd found his way into the driver's seat of my car, while I was consumed with all that had just happened, mixed with realizing how close I am to my home.

I don't speak a word to him.

In a relaxed fashion, he jerkily adjusts the seat back and swings his arms over his head. A few minutes later, he is snoring.

I turn away from him, but I don't want to stir up trouble. I am stuck, or at least think I am stuck and that is ultimately all that matters.

I stay in the same position for the next three hours. I don't change positions until I see the first sign of daylight: leaning against the passenger-side door of the back seat; my head slumped against the door and legs pulled up into my body as far as is humanly possible. I don't bother to put the seat up. I don't have the strength or courage to move from where I was left.

I don't want him to see me. I don't want him to notice me. I don't want to draw any attention to myself. I want to seep through the door, unseen, unheard, gather myself up from the puddle that is now me and erase the timeline from the night before.

My world is upturned and no one will ever know. I'll keep it from creeping into my thoughts. It is easier to blame this all on my drunken escapades than anything else.

In the dewy morning, I walk home. I leave my car parked where it was, a street above my street: too sick to drive. Jarrod, Blaise's water polo teammate, picked him Blaise up on the corner moments before. The haze of the morning seems extra thick this particular Sunday. It's light enough now. I watch my bare feet smack the pavement in a fluid manner, like the bass line of a song. The walk only takes about a minute.

I take a deep breath as I knock on my front door.

The Things People Notice

The next time I see Jessalyn, I ask her why she left that night at Trey's: why I was left alone with Blaise if he was acting insane?

"I was scared. Everyone was scared, even Erol. We didn't know what to do. We didn't know he came back to get you...later."

She looks upset by the question but helpless. Jessalyn wasn't one of my very best friends, but she was definitely in my group of friends. Nevertheless, she seems messed up by the whole thing.

Her eyes dart back and forth, and she continues:

"Jordan told us what happened after prom at Jarrod's. When she tried to help, I mean," Jess says. Jordan is a good friend of Jessalyn and is dating Jarrod's younger brother, Ryan.

"What happened?" I ask.

"Well, Blaise cussed her out, said he'd kill her and stuff... Like I know he was just fucked up and he wouldn't, but he scared her a lot. And we saw the bruises he gave you. Nobody knew what to do," Jess says.

"What the heck! He said that to her?" I look down in shock. "I knew those bruises were from him," I say.

"Kali. We heard him hit you several times. That's why Ryan and Jordan were outside the door that night after prom."

"I thought I fell," I say.

"No, don't you remember? He was shouting at you, something about drinking, and then Ryan said he heard something thud like you'd been thrown or hit. That's when he made Blaise open the door. You guys were in Ryan's room, remember?"

"I remember Jordan asking him to open the door and then Ryan asking if I was okay, but I thought it was because I was drunk. I didn't remember the rest."

"He's bad news, Kali, like very bad news. Be careful," Jess says.

Jay Gatsby: Jaxx Moreau

I knew Jaxx because of his association with the Jayden, Liam group. Jaxx, however, is always somewhat elusive. He was more of an outsider. He was quieter, drunker, taller, calmer, richer, and overall, just more mysterious. Jaxx was the wild card, my favorite. I was fascinated by his persona.

I see him pass by every morning at Break. Our eyes met often, but we never say a word. He dresses like he owns a Maserati, a house in the Hollywood Hills, starred in as well as directs his films and plays in an alternative-rock band in his free time. He is Jay Gatsby to me. Jaxx Moreau puts himself together so well for school; it looks like he doesn't need school at all. He must agree, because he never actually makes it all the way to class.

Among his wardrobe staples are; Jack Purcells, UGG slippers, Tiffany's dog-tag necklace, and multiple pairs of the same style of True Religion Brand Jeans. And he always wore a V-neck: a deep V-neck. I've never even seen Jaxx in a shirt with a standard collar. If he is dressed in a button-down shirt, the first few buttons are undone. I think his cousin taught him this.

His dark-brown faux hawk is always on point: soft looking, but in the perfect place and he is a cool six foot two, not counting the hair. He is my kind of guy. And, he is part Cherokee, so he appreciates my fascination with Native American culture and jewelry. Jaxx is the first guy I become entangled with in an otherworldly type of way. No one understood Jaxx. But this was the guy I would chase.

Jaxx was a star player on the Newport Coast football team, and one of Coach Schuyler's favorite players, just like Maddox. He was forced to quit due to neck and back injuries that plagued him since his near-death DUI accident. It also caused him to have to double up on his chiropractic visits.

Crazy enough, before I knew Jaxx, but knew of him, back in the Z-Boys days, I recognized Jaxx's big black truck wrapped around a street lamp in the Yacht Streets. I had only seen his truck maybe once, if at all, but I remember vividly, going cold, and pointing it out to a fellow party-goer. The tow truck had already arrived. I knew it was Jaxx.

The Yacht Streets are a neighborhood about eight minutes away from mine. I've spent more time in the Yacht streets than my neighborhood. The neighborhood had two separate pool facilities that served the two rival swim teams during the summer. The Yacht Street's several parks and fields served as soccer practice fields during AYSO season, and their baseball diamonds hosted Little League games come springtime. The long grassy stretches were perfect places to bring a new Golden Retriever puppy or to reminisce on when you played Frisbee there as a kid with your dad.

As a kid growing up, living in the Yacht streets was a dream. When high school rolled around things changed. It quickly became apparent that the fact that you could walk to your best friend's house and wave to your boyfriend's mom on the same block would come back to bite you. Word traveled faster than light in the Yacht Streets. It was the hub of gossip. By high school, I was finally appreciative for that the fact that I didn't live in the Yacht Streets. I'd spent years wishing I did and then all at once it was a blessing that I didn't. There should have been a reality show solely based on the rumors started while gazing out the front window in the Yacht Streets of Newport.

Junior Year, my mom got a job at the local chiropractor's office. She mentioned a couple of times: "that one guy whose friends with Jayden came in today."

And then one day she came home with his name.

"Jaxx Moreau," my mom says, standing in my doorway. "Do you know him, Kali?"

Random was the least of it. I was kind of confused as to why she knew him.

"Yes! What? Why? Please don't tell him I said anything." I beg.

"You didn't say anything Kali, so, not a problem. I was just wondering. He comes in a lot," she says. And then half-way down the hall she continues, "He's cute.... super cute."

It was inevitable that I'd run into him at the chiropractor, as I went almost daily due to constant dance injuries. If it wasn't dancing, it was some new sport I'd picked up on the side like the time I mistakenly made the Volleyball team.

I was really bad.

One fine afternoon, I am reading a magazine in the waiting room next to my mom when—Oh my God it's Jaxx Moreau—walks through the lobby.

Jaxx Moreau does things like goes to the chiropractor? With his dad? He has a DAD? Like me?? Jaxx Moreau isn't of a different species that doesn't have parents or rules or health issues or emotions?? He's real?

It quickly became hilarious even to me that I thought Jaxx was like a magical unicorn man, yet he had given me no reason to think of him in that way.

I am obviously showing some awe because my mom chuckles and leans into my shoulder, "You okay Kali?" she laughs. "You know him, don't you? That's that football player who got the DUI."

"Mom, stop!" I whisper.

"What? He can't hear me," she teases, as Jaxx schedules his next appointment at the front desk. "You're right, though. He is really cute. He looks like that one..."

She stops when Jaxx and his father walk past us to leave. His father catches my gaze, purses his lips together and nods his head.

"Hi," Mr. Moreau says curtly.

Jaxx glances at me quickly. His face turns an odd way like he's seen a teacher outside of the classroom or a ghost. He is shocked to see me there. I didn't even think he knew who I was, yet he looks shocked. It is an odd moment.

The Flower Streets

Tessa: Come hang
Me: I'm depressed. I was at a meeting.
Tessa: Seriously come by. Just come by for a bit.
Me: Maybe...for a second.
Tessa: Love you. See you soon. XOXO

It is a chilly Friday evening in Newport, and I am sitting in the parking lot of our community's mega church: Lighthouse. The church is so large that the many buildings, fields, and facilities that make up Lighthouse are appropriately part of Lighthouse Village.

Lighthouse is the church I grew up attending, whether it be for Easter Sunday service, the Christmas tree lighting ceremony, the carnival, the Sunday farmer's market, Lighthouse Church is a world in it of itself; it is magic.

Everything is new, the facilities are all the best of the best. There are multiple live sound stages, and the middle school campus looks like a mix between a Hollywood nightclub and a ritzy resort cabin in Vail. Even the pavement sparkles at Lighthouse.

I attended Sunday school at Lighthouse as a baby. Sunday school progressed into an exciting summer day camp every summer and then sleep away camp with Emma where we slept in Teepees in the mountains. It was my first time away from home for that long. And then, in middle school, Lighthouse hosted Small Groups, the highlight of my week most of the time and the highlight of middle school when I look back. I attended Small Groups every Tuesday with all of my best friends, including Holly and the Jefferson girls along with Tessa, Kendall and their large group of girls. I even traveled to Mexico to build houses with Lighthouse: and most of the high school even if they weren't part of the church. Lighthouse was where I got baptized with my four best friends; Olivia, Kendall, Tessa, and Jessalyn, wearing my favorite Beatles t-shirt: the one with all four members of the band in squares. I love the photograph of us four, soaking wet, at the church that night. I was proud to have branched out from the people I had gone to school with since kindergarten. I had new friends, and they were so much fun.

When I started school at Newport Coast High School, I ran into kids in the hallway that I hadn't seen since Preschool, and ended up becoming great friends with; the vast yet tight-knit community in Newport is incredible. In my first days as a seventh grader, a boy in my grade who'd been a pitcher on an opposing Little League team ran to catch up with me in the hall to apologize for hitting me with a pitch that day we played their team. Of course, I had no recollection of this happening, since I was probably in third grade, he was a cute guy, and we were friends just like that. We ended up walking into the same Honors Biology class.

But, we aren't in middle school anymore, and things have changed.

I race through my memories parked outside the church's middle school campus. I hadn't parked there on purpose, but because it had been the parking lot that I was used to being dropped off at; I would be able to find the location of the AA meeting easiest from this spot.

It had been a good meeting.

I take my UGG Slippers off of the doorframe and thank myself for attending an AA meeting on a Friday night. I am feeling decent. I'm sober. I bet my parents are pleased.

I start the Range and head toward my house.

The Flower Streets are only a minute away from my house, but I don't feel like being social tonight.

As I turn the corner down my street, I get a rush.

Fuck it.

I U-turn and drive back out of my neighborhood toward the beach. Within a couple minutes, I'm parked out front of the kickback.

It's definitely not a big party. A few people are coming in and out holding red cups, but it's quiet. The light from within the cute cottage-like home is warm and welcoming. It looks more impressive than the interior of my car, so I take a deep breath, switch off my UGG slippers into clunky zip-up boots and tuck my dark denim into the tops.

I don't know the guy whose house it is, but Tessa had told me it was mellow to come over. It was the same scene as every kickback; lots of alcohol, bottles deep, neatly set up in the kitchen next to Solo cups, people smoking weed somewhere like the garage and a few people smoking cigarettes in the yard.

Wait! Is that a skate ramp?

I feel a bit awkward without a drink to shield me as I walk past unfamiliar faces on my way out to the yard. I see a couple of upperclassmen guys sitting at an outdoor table set and head over. I knew them well enough that I didn't feel weird being there if I was talking with them.

Tessa runs by holding the hand of a blonde girl named Kaelani. Kaelani is Tessa's "other" side. They do stuff together that I'll never know about, and don't really care to know about. Kaelani comes from the same sort of background as Tessa and seems to be the person Tessa goes to in order to feel normal. On the negative end of this friendship is the fact that they aren't good girls when they're together, and Tessa ignores me and everyone else as well. She'd often leave me at her grandparent's house on Agate to visit Kaelani, who lived a few streets over. They'd smoke together or something. Kaelani never looked me in the eye. She was disrespectful when I tried to talk to her too. She'd hardly ever respond, and I'm not sure if that's what she did with everyone, or if I was exceptionally irritating to her. Kaelani treated me like dirt.

I didn't gel with many of Tessa's Beach friends. The other side of the Bay is a different place. And Kaelani's attitude problem is cliché.

Is that Jaxx?

I debate going back inside the house, but don't want to be a coward. And don't want anyone to see me turn around and come off like a freak. Jaxx is facing the opposite side of the yard; he's the only one with his back toward me. I say hello to Liam and Tanner and then awkwardly say a few random things.

I wish I was drunk.

Jaxx turns around in his seat, a cigarette in between his fingers as he types into his phone with the same hand. He looks up, sees me and puts the phone down. To my surprise, he gets up.

What is he doing?

"Hi, Kali. Nice to see you," Jaxx gives me a hug and then joins me standing next to the other boys.

Phew, no more awkward standing behind Jaxx trying to make conversation with Liam. Yuck.

I notice a liter-sized Fiji water bottle, my favorite water, on the patio table and also notice that Jaxx is sober tonight or at least, not drunk. He seems nicer than usual and also more, well, happy.

I excuse myself to head back inside, overextended by the appearance of Jaxx and the coinciding conversation. I need to regroup.

Once I'm inside, though, the front door is calling my name. As I'm about to pull the knob toward me, the door opens, a group pours in. I should probably text Tessa and tell her I'm leaving, even if she's in a Kaelani bubble.

There is a white Pottery Barn sofa in the front room of the house across from the big front window and front door. No one is around. I sink into the deliciously comfortable cushions of the sofa to write the text.

Me: *I'm heading out*

I begin to write the text but get lost for a moment, daydreaming about this charming house.

These hardwood floors! I want a little cottage like this...

I am just about to send the text when Jaxx peers around the corner.

"Kali!" he says, "I was hoping you didn't leave yet. Can I sit there?"

"Ha yeah, of course."

What is happening right now?

"I feel like it's been a while," Jaxx says, taking a seat next to me on the sofa and placing his cell phone and Fiji water on the natural wood coffee table in front of the couch.

He outstretches his arms along the back of the cushions and rests one white Chuck Taylor on the table's edge before looking directly into my eyes.

Well, this is interesting.

"It has? Huh," I say. I look away for a moment, taken by surprise by his friendly demeanor and solid eye contact. But when I look back up at him I'm immediately relaxed.

I know him. Even though I don't really know Jaxx, I feel like I've known him forever.

We spend the next hour and a half laughing as drunk people file out of the house and onto the next place. We are in our own world.

Both of us are sober and both as we have just established with one another, are single. One beautiful girl comes over to say good-bye to him, apparently wanting him to ask her to stay, she sits on the arm of the sofa, and looks at him then me saying a few meaningless comments before feeling Jaxx's ice-cold vibe toward her. He shifts his body to face mine directly.

She gets the point.

"Okay, well bye Jaxx. Text me, okay?"

"Later!" Jaxx shouts without her.

"Are you like...?" I hesitate to ask about the girl once she leaves.

He smiles.

"No," Jaxx says quickly, guessing my question before I ask it entirely.

Twenty minutes later Tessa and Kaelani fall into the front room laughing and then Kaelani sees us.

"Wha-hoh! What's going on in here?" Kaelani shouts.

She grabs Tessa's arm so that Tessa stops before walking out the door.

"Whoa! Hey, Guuuuuys! What are you two lovebirds doing?" Tessa says.

She looked shocked at first glance.

We laugh.

"Love you Tessa, have a good night," Jaxx says.

"Love you Boo, be good," Tessa says.

I get up to hug my best friend before she leaves.

"Lady!" she says glancing over at Jaxx and then back to me, "You good? Do you need a ride?"

"I'm good, I drove. Call me tomorrow, I miss you" I say. I really did always miss Tessa. She was a piece of me.

"Love you!" Tessa shouts from the steps outside.

"Bye Kaelani!" I yell. Kaelani had already excited.

"Bye Girl!" I hear faintly from outside. '

Jaxx looks so comfortable on the couch. I don't think twice about staying at the house when I see him there. I want to ask him questions all night. I could hear a group of people still hanging out in the backyard, so I don't feel we're overstepping our stay.

"I have a very important question for you," Jaxx says, looking at his Chuck Taylor sneakers for a moment for effect, "Can I take you to dinner finally?"

Bayside Restaurant

J axx won my parents over the night he picked me up for our first date. They were shocked. He addressed them using our last name and assured them no alcohol would be around when "Kali's with me. I'll keep her safe. I promise."

It's not like this is something they asked him; he just introduced himself by saying that. I went weak at the knees but finally made it down the hall from my room to where Jaxx was waiting, holding a dozen red roses, a white dress-shirt poking out of the sleeve of his sports coat. His shiny Mercedes Benz sedan is parked out front.

I reminisce back to our first date and Jaxx standing in my doorway.

"You look beautiful, Kali," Jaxx says looking past my parents and right into my eyes.

"Thank you. You look good too." I laugh awkwardly.

As I grab the roses from him, my parents are speechless.

"Oh, please come in!" My mother snaps back into the present.

Jaxx reaches down to remove his shoes as he enters.

"You're too sweet. You don't have to do that. This floor has been around since before Kali. Well actually, exactly since Kali. We moved in the week after she was born—"

"Michelle, let's let them relax a bit," my dad says observantly.

He always does that well.

"Oh, sorry! Yes! Come in and relax," my mom says.

She turns to me, as my dad comes downstairs.

"Oh my god Kali, he's so romantic," my mom says between clenched teeth as I whip past her in my favorite white pea coat. I'm a bit embarrassed, but mostly proud, of my very sophisticated date. My mom is still holding the red roses, frozen between the front door and the living room.

"Hi Jaxx, how are you, I'm Kali's dad, Atticus," my father says in one stretched-out sentence as if to present himself, to make sure Jaxx knew who he was dealing with. (He told me later that Jaxx had a good handshake. This review is not given out frequently. There were even people my father disliked immediately due to their handshake.)

"Good to meet you, Atticus, and thank you for letting me take your daughter out to dinner. I'll keep her safe. You have my word."

"Yeah," my dad say, surprised by the courtesy. "So I heard you got a bit lost finding the house?"

Jaxx laughs, "Yeah, just a bit."

"Kali isn't the greatest at giving directions," looking over at me, "huh, sweetie?" he jokes.

I frown back at him and my mom chimes in.

"We are both pretty directionally challenged," my mother adds. "You guys should head out before the place closes!" She wasn't used to 8 p.m. dinner dates.

"Aw, it will be no problem. They know we're coming."

My mother has no response to this statement, because unless he is someone special, Bayside isn't going to stay open an extra hour.

"Would you like something to drink? Not alcohol of course." She laughs uncomfortably.

"That won't be an issue. I don't drink, and I will make sure there is no drinking going on when I'm with your daughter. I thought we'd head out pretty quickly. I made the reservation for seven, and they can be weird," Jaxx explains confidently.

I realize that my mother, for once, was right about dressing up.

"Perfect," I assure him.

"It was so good to meet you—well, the last thing you said was the best part. We appreciate no alcohol being involved," my mother says.

My father chimes in, "Good to meet you Jaxx."

Gatsby Saves the Day with Denim

Jaxx Moreau: Can you make some time for me...maybe like next Wednesday night?
Me: Yes
Jaxx: Finally
Jaxx: Pick you up at 8?
Me: Perfect
Jaxx: Cool. I want to take you Christmas shopping.
Me: Whaaaa?
Jaxx: Relax. Look forward to seeing you.

Just as he said, next Wednesday night I went out with Jaxx. The doorbell rings and my mom answers before I can make it down the hallway.

"Hello, Jaxx. How are you?" my mom says.

"Hey, Mrs. Wheeler. You like nice today," says Jaxx.

"You're too sweet. Come on in. I'll get Kali," she walks toward the hallway and shouts, "KAA-oh! Sorry, I didn't see you there Angel," she says and then says to me, out of Jaxx's view, "and he comes to the door every time? I love this guy."

Jaxx takes me to a sample sale hosted by a friend of his in the Yacht Streets. The house is on the corner of Derrick's street; I realize as we turn the corner and park.

Derrick, Brooks, and several other juniors are drinking from red cups outside. It's a mix of adults and teenagers carrying designer jeans over their shoulders.

This means Jaxx, and I are dating publicly.

Did he do this on purpose?

It dawns on me that the entire party would see us together. It's a Wednesday night; friends don't take opposite gender friends to sample sales to try on pairs of their favorite jeans.

Inside, I realize it's less weird than I'd imagined a sample sale with the guy I have a crush on would be. Most people are drunk, including adults. And I'm surprised at how many people I know. I'm hugged from behind from a dozen upperclassmen girls who are also there picking our jeans and dressed in Christmas sweaters.

Once again, I am shocked by Jaxx's normality. He respectfully greets Brooks' mom, who is hosting the sale, and in return, she gives me a long drunk hug and stares at him with drunken cougar eyes.

A friend of mine from dance, Kenna, grabs my hand.

"Girl!" she says, pulling me into the other room which has baskets full of True Religion, Seven and Cloth and Crown denim.

As I am gushing about how much I love the True Religions I just put on, Jaxx enters and snatches the two other pairs off of my shoulder.

"I'll be right back," Jaxx says. He walks away, stops, and turns around, "Wait, do you like those too?"

"What? These jeans? I love them! But no—"

"Ssshh, it's Christmas, and they look really good on you. Just change real quick and throw that pair over to me," Jaxx says.

I rush behind the makeshift changing area to throw him this third pair. I'm speechless.

New Years with Jaxx and the Beach Crew

This New Year's Jaxx invited me to a party at his best girlfriend, Kelsey's place in Baycrest.

Kelsey is from the other side of the Bay, Newport Beach High School: "Beach." It's rougher at Beach. Probably because it's a bigger school, it's only a high school, and it pulls from a larger population than Newport Coast does. Also, the students expelled from Coast get sent to Beach.

Jaxx attended Beach for a year or so after being kicked out of Coast. I never asked him why because I didn't care, I would guess it was probably for skipping class or alcohol. We all did the same stuff; it's just that Jaxx got caught because he wasn't doing well in school and didn't have a home life to come back to at the end of the day. Now, he attends an alternative high school where he takes classes on his schedule.

At Kelsey's, the Senior Girls from Beach all have on New Years mini dresses and stilettos. Louis Vuitton, Marc Jakob, and Michael Kors purses litter the counter, little flasks and Swisher Sweets tumbling out.

The girls are loud when we arrive, and they throw themselves on me to introduce themselves. It's completely unexpected. They are nice to me! After a while, and enough pictures with these girls to collage my entire bedroom with Polaroids, Jaxx rescues me. He grabs my hand as he walks by, snatching me, from the drunken ramblings of Kelsey's friend.

"Thought you might need a break," he smiles.

We both are not drinking. Jaxx leads me through the glass doors and onto the deck. It's pitch-black outside. He leads me through the dark to the pool chairs of Kelsey's Baycrest home. We are far enough above the town that stars are visible. I'm wearing a sparkly "2009" headband. Jaxx has his signature bottle of Fiji. He always carries a liter-sized Fiji water bottle instead of a drinking now. Everything changed for him after his DUI, and it's like I met the updated version of Jaxx that night in the Flower Streets.

I fall for Jaxx because he is refreshing. He is enough not to need to be plastered. He can hold his own at a high school party completely sober. He isn't nervous around me. He calms me down and gives me chills simultaneously.

Dr. Scott M.D. (GP): January 7, 2008
Medications: Synthroid, Lamictal, Topamax
Chief Complaint: Low back pain/abdominal right side. Given note for leg sprain.

The Portofino Journal Revisited

February 02, 2008

It has been about a year since I left Portofino and I am a complete and total mess. Last month ended with my pounding nine beers in my room before Christmas Eve dinner. I was so hung over (puking) that I said I had the stomach flu, and I drunkenly crashed my car into a curb and had to have the tow truck come and haul it away. This is aside from the months and months of blacking out, drinking alone, chipping teeth on vodka bottles, eating napkins, pulling tables over on myself, snorting coke, the list goes on and on. I'm a wreck. I have thirty days sober and have been attending meetings, but honestly, I just want to drink myself to death. (See Appendices F, J.) All I want to do is get an apartment and drink morning until night every day, ALONE. (See Appendices F, J.) XO Kali Rae

Jimi Hendrix and The Intruders: Pre Court Rituals

A few weeks after our first date at Bayside Restaurant, Jaxx is crashing in the spare bedroom next to the garage again. This happened frequently now.

We would often turn on a movie in the great room. I would fall sound asleep in his arms, and he would fall sound asleep wrapping me up in them. I had trouble sleeping most of the time, so it was refreshing for my mother to see my actually resting for once. My mom said it warmed her heart the way he held me. She frequently took pictures of us sleeping. She thought it was impressive that we could get comfortable and stay asleep like that.

The photographs she took of us two are part of the reason that my she did not kick Jaxx out in the middle of the night. He was just a kid, it would seem cruel to make him go home at that hour. So, sometimes my mom woke him up to move into the office bedroom. Most of the time, she didn't bother.

It's ironic to think that the mixture of opiates, Xanax and Somas may have been part of the reason for the coziness. It was such a beautiful thing to see from the outside, but were we disasters on the inside: I particularly, was a walking black box warning. (See Appendices B, R, S.)

"Kali, tonight, I'm Jimi Hendrix," Jaxx says.

"Cool! Why?" I ask.

"I'm going to be put in jail tomorrow. I may be in there for six months. Why not?" Jaxx says.

"I feel you," I say.

My heart aches remembering that this starry-eyed model had been charged with possession and intent to sell narcotics before ever having met me.

"You ready?" Jaxx asks.

He sets down the brown paper bag he is carrying. I come with him to the car to grab his suit.

"You ironed your suit, right?" I ask.
"Duh. Do you even know who I am?" Jaxx replies.
"Uh, yeah, I think...," I say.
"Who do you think I am?" Jaxx asks.
"Jaxx Mor—" I begin.
"Wrong! I'm Jimi!" Jaxx shouts.

He reaches into the back seat of his jeep to grab his Pineider calfskin duffle bag.

Later that night, my father gets home, carrying three bags of Italian takeout. Jaxx swings around the corner. My mom and I are talking at the bar in the kitchen.

"Hello, Mr. Wheeler!"

"Oh, hey there, Jaxx, nice shirt."

Jaxx has on green corduroy bell-bottoms and a dark purple, paisley, button-up shirt, unbuttoned almost to his belly-button.

"Oh my God, he was serious!" I shout, as my mom and I erupt into a fit of giggling like schoolgirls.

It's the night before Jaxx's court date, the spring of my Junior Year, Jaxx's Senior Year. Things have been a bit rough for Jaxx lately. His brother had recently got into trouble with the law and the elementary school-aged boy was now going to Juvenile Hall. His father kicked him out of the house, depending on his mood that day, and his mother is struggling with an addiction that just reared its head again. My parents offer up the office bedroom.

Recently, I could not get a hold of Jaxx by any means: friends, social media, his mother, no one knew where he had gone. No one could find him, and his mother texted me to see if I was possibly him. A few days later, the cops found him at his mother's new apartment building, passed out on a neighbor's porch. He was messed-up on drugs; asking for his mother: if they knew where she had been.

He left his father's house, after a group of mobsters showed up repeatedly, asking him for money and threatening Jaxx if he did not pay up. Jaxx explained the men as mob men of a sort. They stopped him on multiple occasions while he was getting in his car to come back to Newport. His father lived inland quite a bit.

One of the stories I remember clearly had to do with these same men surprising him by coming up the ivy side of his dad's house. They climbed up the hill from the street below the home. One man had a bat. And they wanted "the money"—confused Jaxx managed to dodge the main guy and slam the door of his car before two more men in white jackets are made visible by his headlights.

The stories are terrifying. And the way he explains them to me, no matter what is going on, Jaxx's fear is real.

Around 2 a.m., Jaxx wakes me up.

"They were in your front yard just a minute ago," Jaxx says.

"Oh my God! Are you serious?" I crack open the shutters that looked straight out over our lawn. "This is terrifying! Where did they go?"

"I don't know, but I don't feel comfortable with you in your bedroom alone. What if those men come in through the side door?" Jaxx says.

"How many were there?" I ask.

"I saw three, but I heard the garage door being shaken, so there could have been more guys doing that," Jaxx says.

"Is everything okay, Guys?" my dad asks, standing in the doorway of the guest bedroom; his eyebrows furrowed.

"Mr. Wheeler, I think we have a problem. We need to call the police." Jaxx says.

"Wait, what? What's going on?" my dad says.

"There were four men in your front yard," Jaxx says. "I think I've seen them before."

"Do you know them?" my dad says.

"No, but they threatened me. I saw those same guys at my dad's house," Jaxx says.

"Wait, hold on. Are they trying to rob us? Do they want to speak to you?" my dad asks. He's worried now.

"I have no idea. I don't know what I'd be talking with four strangers about. I thought I saw one guy carrying a bat," Jaxx says.

"Kali, go upstairs and lock the door," my dad says.

"Okay," I reply.

I run up the stairs and slide the glass door shut, click.

My mom wakes up and asks, "Kali Rae, what's going on?"

"Jaxx saw a group of men outside," I say.

"Call the cops! There have been two break-ins this year on our street!" My mom shouts.

She clicks the bedroom light on and throws the white comforter off her.

"Michelle—don't call anyone yet. Jaxx is going to check it out. I don't see anyone there," my dad shouts from downstairs.

"Dad! You can't let him go out there!" I say.

"Kali, he has a bat. He's a big guy. There shouldn't be an issue. I'm grabbing my cell phone, just in case. Michelle—put the phone down. Let's not jump the gun," my dad says.

She was indeed holding the phone.

Jaxx went out front to investigate and found no one. We don't have street lamps, so it's dark and downright dumb to stay out there looking for trouble. My father retreated up the stairs to sleep with my mother, giving us both strict instructions to call the cops if we saw anyone out there again.

About twenty minutes later, Jaxx is in my room.

"Yeah, they're back, " Jaxx says. He's freaked out.

"Okay, stay here. The doors are locked. Call the police. Tell them what you saw, " I saw.

After about thirty minutes of intense inner investigation--head in hands, alternating to hands-on-knees, shaking his head while sitting on the bed in the office, Jaxx decides the best and most logical thing to do is to alert the police of the possible intruders.

The cops come and take a statement from Jaxx at my front door. It is now 4 a.m.; my parents are exhausted.

They cops leave only after carefully checking the perimeter of the house. We don't have to be involved. It takes an hour for the bright flashlights to stop shining through various windows of our house. I fall back asleep in Jaxx's arms. It is against the rules, but Jaxx is worried about having me so far away (a bedroom away).

Jaxx is convinced that there are mobsters outside and doesn't want them entering through the side-door between my bedroom and the office and kidnapping me in my sleep.

Upon gaining distance from the situation, it becomes clear that the men were very likely hallucinations due to the painkillers, anti-anxiety, and ADHD medication-tonic that Jaxx was sipping.

Apparently Jaxx took more pills than usual, nervous for his court date in the morning.

I didn't think that was a possibility at the time. I knew Jaxx was messed up, but I had no idea it would span as far as making him delusional, and causing him to hallucinate actual people in my yard.

It came together when I was explaining to my mother why he had wanted to stay at our house. I explained to her the men that tried to jump him outside his dad's house. My mom immediately blurts out, "Is he on drugs?"

I thought it was rude of her to blame it on drugs. But when I went to explain things the way that Jaxx had described them to me, I just sounded nuts. When Jaxx told it to me, his emotions about the situation made it real for me too. However, with the emotions removed, it sounded like a drug addict's hallucination.

Dr. Morano: February 04, 2008
Lamictal
*??
Dr. Morano switches the subject when asked about the notes from this day and his notes are not readable

Dr. Fiaschetti M.D. (psychiatrist): March 21 2008
Zoloft 50mg added for depression

"Inappropriately Sexual": Disagreements with Mom

I couldn't recall the effects of Zoloft until I read the notes Dr. Fiaschetti took: "Became inappropriately sexual" and it all rushes back to me.

My mother accompanies me into Dr. Fiaschetti's office today. I absolutely hate when she does this, but she is adamant, and because I am not a legal adult, I have to allow it.

The two large leather sofas allowed me to have some room from my overbearing mother. Before I can say a word, my mom chimes in, "This one isn't good. She's been acting funny, inappropriately sexual, making comments about sex a lot," she says, Dr. Fiaschetti is already scribbling on her legal pad.

"Are you kidding?" I say, "Mom, it was a joke. It's a rap song."

More frustrated than I'd been in a while, I try to un-explain what my mother has just told the doctor.

"I was playing around. I don't feel anything with this drug," I say.

"Yes you do," my mom says under her breath. She's crossing her arms over her chest, and ducking her chin into her sternum, assuming her passive-aggressive, under-the-breath-comments position.

"How would you ever know how I feel?" I say quickly.

"Okay Guys, let's just stop this one. We can try another," Dr. Fiaschetti says hoping to defuse the situation.

"Wait, why!" I shout.

"Good," my mom says.

"Kali, because there are better choices. And if it's affecting your behavior—," the doctor says.

"And this is why I don't like my mom here with me. I was quoting a rap song in the car. This is ridiculous. I—" I say.

"No, Kali, you were also watching that reality show: that raunchy one," my mom says.

"Is this comedy?" I say, actually pissed off now as the Nurse Ratched feeling is bubbling back up.

Dr. Fiaschetti is already flipping through the five-inch-thick, dictionary-size, prescription index.

"Let's try something new," Dr. Fiaschetti says, smiling as she leans up against her maple wood desk.

After looking into Zoloft, it is ironic that I would want to stay on this one since it's effectiveness is likened to a sugar pill. (See Appendix M.)

Dr. Morano M.D. (psychiatrist): March 03, 2008
Seroquel and Topamax
Off of Lamictal
Samples of Effexor

Dinners with Gatsby

Jaxx takes me out to dinner almost every night. Our default spot is a sushi place down the street from my house. We are there probably five times a week, most weeks. We always order the same things. Jaxx gets the barbecue pork combo plate, and I get unagi: the Japanese word for freshwater eel. It is my favorite food.

He always orders extra eel sauce, grinning at the waitress like he is asking his mother for the go-ahead to have dessert before dinner. It is the same thing, every night, the same way, with extra eel sauce.

Jaxx sticks to his side of the bento box for about a year, until I manage to get him to try eel, leading to a slight shift: "extra eel sushi as well," he now adds.

The hostess and the sushi chefs know our names and our preferred table. They always bring me out a Diet Coke to start the night. I take the Norco Jaxx has for me right when he arrives to pick me up. I chew them to make sure I get the most out of it. The sour grit stays stuck in my molars until the Diet Coke rinsed some of it out.

It starts with Jaxx allowing me to have half, and later a couple and then just a few, but it increases rapidly to seven. Within months, I spend the entire night coaxing him into letting me have more Norco or a sip from the Norco water that he hid somewhere in the Mercedes. Taking eleven Norco in one night is standard now, just to feel well enough to make it through the night.

We learn to time things out so that we experience the greatest high. Without a word of it, Jaxx and I would starve all day, and take the first dose upon leaving for my house for the restaurant. The next dose we take right as we park behind the sushi place. If we have to wait longer than a few minutes for our food, we will be sick, which is why it is a delicate balance between starving to feel high and being overcome with nausea and vertigo because you forgot to eat and took too many. Upset the balance and an inevitable retching session no matter where you were, would follow; Norco fever was undeniable and unforgiving.

Every day like clockwork, I would develop a migraine. It would finally cease once the medicine took effect. I can tell right when they kick in because the entire restaurant falls quiet: silenced. When I speak, my voice echoes inside my head. Like dominos, the pain ceases, and then I fall madly in love with the man dressed so nicely across the table from me at my very favorite restaurant.

Depending on how Jaxx was feeling that night, we would stall the meal. He would often not eat much at all. My guess was that he was savoring the ride. I did the same thing, but my stomach was weaker than his; often I started sweating with nausea praying for the food to arrive.

It went like this every, single, night.

I introduced Jaxx to a local take-out Italian joint, and its bomb pasta salad. I taught him to mix their house dressing and Italian vinaigrette all together with the tri-colored Rotini, seal the lid, and shake until the pasta soaked up all the tangy goodness. It quickly became his favorite meal. Sometimes we'd splurge and eat a meatball sandwich as an homage to my childhood. But most of the time we did sushi.

Sometimes we ate at the Bay Club. His grandfather has an account there. Jaxx calls Liam, Liam grabs Tessa, and we all meet at the Bay Club on Mr. Weber's dime, with his approval of course.

We spend all night at the piano bar watching wealthy Newport couples dance in their best party attire. We people-watch and construct stories about the lives of the women shrieking out of drunken pleasure as they sip martinis. Liam and Tessa usually took off midway through the night. But we stayed, we had nowhere else to be. And we were both not into the high school scene.

When we got hungry, we would have a late-night dinner on the patio overlooking the Bay, and the yachts parked at their docks. They would open the restaurant for us and bring heat lamps out to the patio at 11:30 at night. They all called him Mr. Weber.

"Hello, Mr. Weber, what will you have tonight?"

"Mrs. Weber," the host nods in greeting. Jaxx doesn't correct him. I shrink in embarrassment, but it's kind of fun. Everything with Jaxx is fun: carefree.

The drugs dissolve into my empty stomach, carefully timed to set in before we fill our bellies, I fall into the moment with Jaxx.

All I see is him. All I hear is his voice. All that I ever want is encompassed, directly or indirectly, within him. He makes all of my pain disappear, every single time.

In each one of the beautifully hazy moments with Jaxx, I felt I could accomplish anything: whatever I dreamt, I could accomplish with Jaxx by my side. Within those moments, no matter the way, I knew we would make it, and we were going to make it big. He had everything I wanted and everything I needed.

I didn't think of logistics; I didn't think of the ways in which things would or would not happen. I didn't focus on figuring out if the only thing that healed me both mentally and physically was bad for me. It didn't matter; I couldn't have cared less because it worked. They were the only thing that had ever worked for me.

Jaxx learns to soak the yellow pills and strain them to separate the hydrocodone from the acetaminophen. This way, he would only eat the hydrocodone side and partially save his liver. It intensified the high. By the end, Jaxx combines Norco with pills that reduce stomach acid and takes everything on an empty stomach. I follow suit. It is supposed to increase their potency. He knew every trick in the book to savor the high of the pain medication.

The path to "80s" (80mg of Oxycontin) paved itself pretty quickly in retrospect. It starts with Vicodin, moves along to Norco and then one evening Jaxx brings something new to the equation: "80s" parked in the back of the same sushi joint.

He sucks off the blue coating, leaving a bit of dye on his lips, and splits the now white pill into two. He hands me half of one-half on the tip of his pointer finger.

"Only this for now. It's really strong, Kali," Jaxx says.

Jaxx never wanted to give me any of his pills, but I persisted. After the first few times, my body adapted to them. Jaxx and I were together every night, so there was never a problem of coming down. Sometimes he slept on this sofa in the great room. We were inseparable. If we were planning to be apart, Jaxx would supply enough medicine for that time.

Usually, though, we would plan to be apart and end up together. Jaxx having driven from whatever he was, no matter the hour, up to my home in the quiet neighborhood of Newport Coast. We were never apart. We even slept intertwined. My mom said she walked in on him once just stroking my hair as I slept; I was ill and he never left my side.

Jaxx Alexander Moreau was the bad boy who had gone "good," at least for me and at least for now. He was my antidote.

Driving into Compton: Witnessing my First Drug Deal

"Please let me come!" I beg Jaxx. I'd been lying on my couch for days after unintentionally withdrawing from a sample Dr. Morano provided me. The Internet explains that I am suffering from "brain shivers." It is just as bad, if not worse, than it sounds. (See Appendix N.)

"Please, please, please," I say.

"Kali, I'm just going to drive there, grab them, and leave," Jaxx says.

"Pleeeease? I've never been to Compton," I say.

"It's not a place you would fit in," Jaxx says.

"Come on! Have some fun. I don't want to sit here all day again. Take me to LA with you!" I beg.

"Fine. Please don't wear those glasses."

I pull the Marc Jacobs white and gold aviators out of the hair on the top of my head. We'd just taken a walk, and I was too sick to notice I'd left them on.

"Why?" I ask.

"Kali you realize this is not a joke right? We are driving into the ghetto," Jaxx says.

"Cool! I'm down! Let's take your Jeep, though."

He laughs. "Yeah, we will be taking the Jeep for sure."

A text comes through on his phone. "Okay, let's go. He's waiting," Jaxx says.

I am thrilled.

We will be picking up an entire bag of Norco. Most are to sell, and they sell for ten dollars each. It is as if we are retrieving a lottery prize with a raffle ticket.

Plus, it means we can take as many as we want for a few days until it's time for him to divide them up and sell them.

The thought of the surplus is mouth-watering. I imagine driving to West LA, maybe somewhere like Playa Vista, and then accompanying Jaxx into someone's house to retrieve the pills before thanking everyone and driving back to Newport.

An hour later, we are outside a dilapidated house. The lawn is dead and the window-curtains don't even cover the entire window. It is like a movie set to me.

Do people live in there?

"You need to duck down. He doesn't know you're here," Jaxx says.

"What the hell. Tell him!" I say.

"Kali, you don't get it. Just climb into the back seat," he says.

I realize the seriousness of the request in his tone and follow directions.

"Kali...Go!" I hear confident fear in his tone.

Huddled on the floor mat behind the passenger seat, I listen to a couple yelling.

"Oh shit!" Jaxx says, very seriously, "Fucking cops. Are you goddamn kidding me?"

"Duck down!" he whisper-yells at me.

"Is it a goddamn block fucking party?" he says in the same muffled tone. "Oh fuck. We are so fucked. Fuck. Do NOT get up."

I have no idea what is going on. I hear a group of people arguing. Their voices are getting closer.

A man says something to Jaxx...

"Waiting for Andre," Jaxx says.

"The fuck are you?" the man asks.

"Just picking something up, Man," Jaxx repeats.

"You need to get outta here, Boy," the man says.

At this point, I am sweating profusely. I don't know if there's a gun pointed at Jaxx's head, or if we are in a different city now or if this is a cop. (It doesn't sound like a cop.)

"Hey, boys, what are you doing?"

Now THAT sounds like a cop.

I'm more scared now than I was before. I hear feet hitting the pavement in tennis shoes. Whoever was talking with Jaxx must have run off.

"Hello, Officer. Can you help me get back to the 405?" says Jaxx.

"Sure," he says hesitantly. "Where are you coming from?" the officer responds.

I can hear his radio rattling off different police codes and cross-streets. The white noise static adds to the terror of this equation.

"A club that I promote up in West Hollywood, but I need to get back to Orange County," Jaxx say.

"Far way from there, you know. Take a couple of lefts and ride that street all the way down to the Rite Aid on the corner," says the officer.

"Thank you, Officer."

I exhale.

Thank God. I feel the car start to move and am finally aware of why he didn't want me here.

"Are we bailing on the stuff?" I ask in a whisper.

"Don't talk to me right now," Jaxx says back through clenched teeth.

"Dammit. He is on the corner of the street over. We've got to meet him. He's waiting," says Jaxx.

I am mad nor surprised. I want to pick up the Norco.

"Is it safe?" I ask.

No answer.

"Hey!" I hear an unfamiliar voice. "Drive down to the red house over there; it's not chill here," the man says.

I then hear Jaxx flip through the hundred-dollar bills he has rolled up in his pocket.

"No shit," Jaxx says.

"Bro put that away. Now! Not chill," the man says again.

We drive for a few minutes and after a moment of being stopped and the sound of a brown bag and the rattle of pills along with, "Nice. Thanks, bro."

The window rolls up.

"Stay down, I'll drive to the store, and we can get something to eat before we head back," he says.

"It's over?" I ask.

"Stay down, Babe."

A few minutes later:
"YEAH BABBBBBBY! We got them!" Jaxx shouts.

He's holding a paper lunch sack filled with two one-gallon plastic bags full of yellow, oblong pills.

Dr. Fiaschetti M.D. (psychiatrist): April 18, 2008
Seroquel up to 100mg for insomnia/mania (See Appendix I.)

Three Bars

My mother and I were traveling to visit my sister's new school. The night before I left, Jaxx came over with a care package. He packed a group of pills in a little plastic baggy that I could stuff in my wallet.

"I don't want to leave you," I say.

"You'll have fun. You're only gone for ten days, " Jaxx replies.

"Yeah, but I'll miss you."

"Take these. You'll be fine."

"Well, you look bigger!" Kayla says the moment we are reunited in Pennsylvania.

Back in the hotel room, I fumble through my suitcase to find the little bag of assorted pills. I need to take something to rid myself of the nausea that's beginning to consume me.

I take a total of three bars of Xanax before dinner.

I took the first Xanax bar on the train, which made for a fabulous picture: me, slumped over against the train window in a full down parka, hair everywhere (it looked like I had been shot). You can't tell from that picture if I am asleep, or dead. And actually, I couldn't cared less about killing myself via benzos at the time.

I learn that we have to go to dinner with my sister and her boyfriend that night. So, I decide I need a two-hour nap beforehand to refresh. I take another Xanax bar to sleep and to prepare myself for Kayla. We'd been close growing up, but all of a sudden she started acting like I was the enemy.

She hated me.

I wake up to Kayla shouting at me that we're late. I'd slept for two and a half hours according to her yelling. I don't respond, or get up, so my mother comes over. they both stand by the bed jostling me.

I am pissed off that Kayla, and my mom now, are forcing me out of out of these insanely comfortable hotel sheets. I feel fat, and I'm crabby. This is going to be a long night.

I fumble through my suitcase again and take half a Xanax bar to motivate me to jump into the shower.

It bothers me that Kayla said I looked fat, and it bothers me even more that her boyfriend never spoke. It is awkward to have dinner with someone who hardly speaks, except baby talk to Kayla. It bothered me the most that Kayla had been a jerk to me since 7th grade. I take another half of a Xanax bar to shove all the boiling emotions back down.

I remember dinner is dark and I eat pasta: nothing else.

My mom tells me a couple of weeks later, that I slept through that dinner. I slurred my speech so badly when I tried to order angel hair bolognese (solid choice) that she had to help order for me. And then, after I finished the pasta, I tried to order it again.

She said I ate with my face so close to the bowl that, "I thought you might fall in, like fall into the bowl, Kali."

Dr. Morano's Mental Break: My Psychiatrist Was Tased

We pull up to Dr. Morano's office a few minutes early, but as we arrive, we both see a very strange thing. The windows are boarded up.

"What the heck," my mom stops the car and we both get out.

The doors are locked, and there is a single, 8 ½ by 11 sheet of paper that reads:

"Dr. Morano is no longer working here. We apologize for the inconvenience."

We look at each other in sheer disbelief. Is this a movie?

"What the heck. I guess you aren't going in for an appointment today. What are we supposed to do? There's no number!" my mom says.

"I don't know..." I say, completely grayed-over. "Call the old number."

The drugs put me in a constant dead zone. I would stare through the window of the car, and then I'd stare somewhere else when we got out. I couldn't feel things like normal. For instance, when we were moments away from being T-boned by a car in an intersection, I didn't even flinch. I felt already dead inside.

I come back to and see my mother on her cell phone.

"Yes. Hello, this is Michelle Wheeler; my daughter Kali Wheeler has an appointment today with Dr. Morano, and the building is boarded up. What are we supposed to do?" she says.

She paces in the empty parking lot. It's pretty early, so there aren't many people there at all. The morning dew is chilling. It reminds me of the suffocating feeling of being in school.

"Yes, I see that. Because I am here at the office for my daughter's appointment today and I am reading the sign you have on the door. And that's what the sign says. Can you tell me more? Like why? And also where I'm supposed to take my daughter...Okay. That sounds great. Thank you so much," my mom says, hanging up the phone, turning to me, "Kali, this is so strange. The nurse is calling Dr. Morano's cell phone number to get the address of his new office. She won't tell me anything." My mom shakes her head, and continues, "This is too weird. Maybe he's taking his own meds."

"Probably," I say.

"Well, let's head home I guess. Shoot. I took you out of school too."

A couple of moments later, her phone rings.

"Yes! Oh hi, Dr. Morano, I'm okay how are you? Okay, now? Okay, and what number is it again? Great, we will head over," my mom says into the phone. "Let's go!" my mother shouts at me.

I'm still studying the odd-looking boards in the windows.

"It's not like there's a hurricane coming. Why did they board it?" I ask.

"Kali, I have no idea, but we've got to go. I have a new address for him, and he says he'll see you today. We might as well take advantage of having the day off," my mom says.

The new office is odd. The building is new. The pavement is so white that it would certainly cause eye damage if you stared at it, particularly at this hour. The building looks nice enough. We are both pleasantly surprised.

The waiting room is a whole lot smaller than Dr. Morano's first office. His normal office took up the entire first floor of a large corporate office; flat-screens lined the waiting room and the file cabinets behind the nurses were bookshelves. But this waiting room only has six chairs, two of which are taken up by two men who look as if there is no way in hell they are from Newport or even Orange County.

The closest thing I can relate them to is a cross between farmers and construction workers. Both men are missing teeth and talking in the growly, Midwestern, I just smoked two packs of Marlboro's-tone, and they are talking so quickly.

The guy closest to me has on a baseball cap that looks as if he hasn't taken it off... ever. They are unshaven, unkempt and their eyes bulge. The guy nearest me is bouncing his leg so intensely that the entire floor is vibrating with it. I am sufficiently freaked out.

My mother and I sit there silently. When one of the guys is called back, Dr. Morano comes out to get him. There are no nurses, no sign-in sheet, nothing. The other man stays behind, bouncing his leg so furiously and flipping through a magazine as if he has been ordered to slap the page down so loudly that it almost makes me jump every time.

I spend the entire forty-five-minute wait time looking at the ground and passing glances to my mother to see if she understands how messed up these guys are; I was honestly terrified. I'd never seen crack addicts, but I am pretty sure these guys are on some very "old-school bad" shit.

Their work boots are so dirty that I wonder where they even came from; it isn't dirt, but stains from overall wear and tear. The sweat pants of the guy who stayed behind are stained with god-knows-what.

Finally, the door to Dr. Morano's office (I'm guessing) opens. The jeans-wearing crazy is shown out of the room, as tweaky as before.

"Thanks, Doctor. Thank you," he stammers.

He's carrying a doggy bag and throws his hand up, addressing my mom and me as he leaves.

"Okay, Kali, let's do this," Dr. Morano say, smiling from the doorway.

I push myself out of the chair and cautiously follow him into the room. It's huge and empty. There is a leather sofa right in the middle of the studio-apartment-sized space. He has a Container Store plastic set of removable drawers next to a comfy-looking leather chair across from the couch. He sits down and crosses his legs.

"Have a seat. Tell me what's up," Dr. Morano says.

His eyes are red. He seems off.

After Blaise and Jaxx, I could smell drugs from a mile away. And this guy was on something. Or, he is legitimately nuts.

His words are so fast, and his thoughts so inarticulate, that the most I can do is smile and nod and try to get in a: "Yeah, sure. I—" before he cuts me off with ideas, options and the opening and closing of the tacky plastic drawers, which I now find to contain what looks like hundreds of different drug samples.

He has a white paper bag that he is placing the medications in as he scribbles something down. Within five minutes, we are done. I leave with one white paper bag, crumpled at the top (like children do with their lunch bags), and another plastic bag filled with samples branded by a large logo of the coinciding pharmaceutical company. My instructions are to try them and report back. The speed with which he gives me these instructions is enough to alert me not to take anything this man had given me.

My mom looks worried.

"So can you tell me what she has here?" she asks a manic Dr. Morano.

"Just a few things that I think will do the job. I think they will help. Yeah, I mean, just some GABA inhibitors, an ancient manic-depressive pill, the original mood stabilizer. It's been around forever and a sample of some Lyrica because I know the pain is hard. Any questions?"

"Why did you move?" my mom asks.

"Aw you know. Things weren't working out. I wanted my own space," he says.

He's sweating through his Trojan Hawaiian shirt, and his khakis look like they have not been ironed in weeks, or he's worn them for multiple days.

"Awesome," my mom says. She's obviously confused, but he can't tell. "Thank you, Dr. Morano."

"Oh and please make the check out to me personally, we can send it through insurance after everything has gone through," he adds.

"Oh!" she turns around, "Why?"

"Easier that way, it's hard with insurance companies, you know," he trails off.

"Well, I need to be going through insurance," she says.

"You know what? Never mind. I can bill them and charge you later, " Dr. Morano says.

"Oh. Okay—" My mom laughs out of discomfort. "See yah!"

"Have a good day! I'm glad you found the place!" Dr. Morano says.

"What the..." my mom starts the moment we bust out of the double doors into the parking lot.

"Mom, no," I warn under my breath, as I see the two men that had been in the waiting room leaning on the cement wall by the exit.

We both smile cordially.

After we shut the doors to her BMW and are safely locked inside away from this entire situation, my mother exhales.

"My God, that was weird," she says.

"You know those guys were addicts, right, Mom? Like, I know those guys were drug addicts."

"Really? They were weird. I think Dr. Morano had a mental break," my mom says.

"I'm never going back there. Those guys were on drugs, and Dr. Morano is too; that, or he's legitimately nuts," I say.

"Okay. I'm okay with that," she says.

Dr. Morano M.D. (psychiatrist): May 05, 2008
Last visit with Dr. Morano
Lamictal
Seroquel
Off of Effexor
*Assorted samples that are not noted

Let's See About Tomorrow: The New Journal

May 20, 2008

I can't finish hanging up my clothes. I'm drunk. And all I want is another sip of the whiskey. It's my parent's whiskey. I hid it in my underwear drawer. I swear it's calling me... that destructive taste...

I miss the Klonopin Jaxx gave me. I miss the Xanax too. I didn't even like the Somas, but I miss them too. I miss the Norco the most. My dealer who happens to be my boyfriend bailed on me.

I want alcohol. I could live with alcohol as my only friend. It's all I want and love. I am alone. I am alone.

My first entry in this new journal, but it's not. I've entered these in my head a million times before. The million times I've sat crying, fucked up alone n whatever I could buy: whatever I could find. Today I don't want to die. I want to sing. This is good. I want to live today. Let's see about tomorrow.

XO Kali Rae

Grandpa Weber's Famous Infinity Pool

When we arrive at Jaxx's grandpa's home, the house doesn't stand out as much as I had imagined. Within the dazzling, oceanfront community, the mansions beside Mr. Weber's modest driveway, dwarf the entrance. The only thing visible is a one story structure and a dark wood fence. Jaxx types in a code and pushes open the heavy dark wood door. The trees are dense making the entrance even more hidden than it is already--set back by the placement of the long driveway taking up three regular sized house lots. There's a coy pond beside the walkway. I spot the sparkling Pacific Ocean through a break in the trees on the side of the house. A wall-sized window set to the right of the front door allows me to see all the way through the several rooms of plush carpets and onto the water. It

Once inside, it's warm: quiet but homey. The carpet is squishy between my toes, having taken my strappy sandals off at the door. A fish tank lines the wall of the room to my right, which serves as an extra dining room or a place to remove your shoes upon entering. There's a small river, the one from the entranceway, running through the four-story cliffside dwelling overlooking the ocean. His home is directly over my favorite rock formation.

Jaxx and I stay in the guest bedroom, which is more like a two-bedroom pool house complete with a master bathroom, huge bathtub, and even robes like a hotel. Our room is on the same level of the home as the infinity pool: three stories down from the entrance and two or so stories above the beach.

I can think of nothing better than to spend my summer lounging on this unbelievably gorgeous deck: the pool and Jacuzzi heated to perfection. It is like being a constant honeymoon. No one is ever around except for his grandpa's new wife, Coraline, who stops by occasionally for a minute or two. It's strange how often the house is only accommodating the different housekeepers that keep the place pristine. There's a chef, too, which is a little bit awkward, especially when I just want to spend an hour touring the kitchen pantry and refrigerator. It's unbelievable: endless supplies of whatever you could possibly want. The stocked fridge in our place is alcohol-free; the alcoholic drinks have been removed strategically and replaced with cold bottles of Fiji Water: heaven.

I change out of my white sundress, noting how soft the carpet is again. I feel underdressed in my bikini and grab a plush towel out of the marble bathroom to throw it over my shoulders before tying back the canvas curtains and sliding the heavy glass door open into the sun. Even the grass poking out of the cracks in the concrete looks technicolor green.

It's July, and the sun is bright. Jaxx is already lounging on one of the chairs by the infinity pool; he's on his phone. As I stand shocked at the interior of the guest bedroom he gets to stay in whenever he pleases.

Jaxx had thrown his keys down nonchalantly, pulled several Norco out of his jeans pocket, plopped them into his water bottle and hid it behind a throw pillow on one of the elegant chairs by the flat-screen. This was a spare.

A gardener is working to the right of the Jacuzzi, trimming the trees that encompass the whole property. It is like a sanctuary. And, from the deck I can look up to see the tier-like levels of the Zen-style property: it's gorgeous.

Wait.

I recognize that Jacuzzi.

Before I can say anything, Jaxx explains.

"Oh yeah, remember that episode with Kasey and Stephen at Stephen's pool?"

"Yeah…" I say.

"They filmed all of that here," Jaxx says.

"Wait…they used your grandparent's house for the show?" I ask.

"Yeah, all the time. That car was ours too, the red one that looked like a toy. That's my grandpa's car; we can take it out if you want," Jaxx says.

Grandpa Weber is a congenial man. If there was a Grandpa to Jay Gatsby, Mr. Weber was the inspiration. And he acted thrilled to see us, even with the knowledge that Jaxx was struggling, he welcomed his grandson with open arms, while smoking a cigar on the desk, pondering the ocean with his nicely combed hair. He was the boss of the family and Jaxx looked up to him as a father.

Jaxx hadn't forgotten to bring two Fiji water bottles and was beginning to make himself (and me, but it was never outright for me—he just shared his, or let me "finish" his and made another) the yellow drink that made every day a holiday: Norco in water. I could live forever right here; the sun beating down, Jaxx looking adorable in his white tee and ripped jeans.

He was perfect to me, just perfect. Everything about him: the way he smelled, the way he held me, the fact that he was pretty much the worst of the bad boys in the county, the fact that I'd picked him up from jail a couple of times, and the fact that he tried so hard not to be the way he was when he was with me.

The one thing that Jaxx got right was showing me that he loved me more than anything else in the world. He loved me more than the drugs, more than the cars, more than the cash, more than his ass hole friends, more than his dreams of being a musician, even more than his own sleep, health, and well-being.

Jaxx loved me through thick and thin, through illness after illness. He never left my side.

Whenever I was sick, or upset or tired, Jaxx was there. It might take him a few hours to arrive, but he always came, and he always held me until I was able to unravel myself from his grasp.

It was unbelievable how much he cared about me. He was such a bad kid, but he was so good to me.

Dr. Fiaschetti M.D. (psychiatrist): July 16, 2008
Ritalin LA 30mg in morning and p.m. if needed
Valium 5mg as needed
Still on Seroquel and Topamax [not noted]
Deplin [not noted]

Poetry & Prescriptions: The Leather Journal

August 09, 2008

I want to run away from everything. I got in another fight with Kayla today. I want out of this. And Jaxx...I don't know. I'm confused and scared, and I don't know what to do except run. WANT OUT OF MY CRAZY BRAIN FUCK. My brother told me that talking to me was like talking to a wall. Maybe I'm better off without you all. I hate longing for Jaxx. That's why I never wanted this, whatever this is.

Numb love
I didn't want to feel this,
like I needed your touch.
I didn't want to feel the ache
in my heart
when you're not around,
or the stab
in my gut,
when you don't call.
But you're never around,
not early enough.
and you never call,
not early enough.
And I know the reasons
are all-wrong.

Your reasons are always
all wrong.
The tears run
down my cheeks
as I decide to let
you go.
You know
I never thought it would come to this.

But I think it's time.
It's finally time.
Is this love?
Or just a cover-up?
another disguise.
I'd like to think I'd be with you forever, Babe,
but I think it's something else
that's making these feelings
come alive.

And I'd love to keep
my numb hand in yours,
and watch the cars,
watch life,
fly by,
but I've got to let go.

Babe, I've got to run.
Because I've got to ride.
But maybe I'll be back
someday.
Please forgive me
for leaving you cold in this bed of lies.

I'll pray you forget me,
and these meaningless nights,
and all the nights you held me,
and I couldn't feel your touch.

I'm numb,
Love,
this is
numb love.

XO Kali Rae

August 11, 2008

So school starts tomorrow, and I'm depressed. I always get very sad the day before school starts. It's very hard for me to adjust to routine and I'm freaking out. I just want to run away. I'm afraid. I feel trapped as if I will be stuck in a box while everyone else is moving on without me.

    I went to Disneyland with Jaxx last night and then spent the night at his house. It was the best night ever! Sparks flew...like always...and they weren't from the cigarettes haha.

    I came home this morning and did a bunch of dumb stuff like cleared out my car, my room, etc. If I keep moving, I don't have time to think and therefore can't be sad. But Jaxx just left, and now I'm here again to think...and I go back to the song I wrote on the page before this.

And I've got questions...

I want this aching pain to go away,
to leave my body for a day.
I want my heart to feel a release;
these tears to flow
this confusion to cease.

Will my mind ever rest?
I ask as I look to the clouds
then I look to your strong
yet pained,
soldier's chest.

Will my heart ever heal?
I ask and grab for your hand,
then I grab for my necklace
nestled deep in the sand.

XO Kali Rae

Part V:
Senior Year

Dr. Fiaschetti M.D. (psychiatrist): September 19, 2008
Seroquel 50mg added for insomnia
Topamax 150mg for migraines
Trileptal 150mg twice/day for mood stabilizer

Groundhog's Day: Let's Try Something—The Same?

In September of my Senior Year, Dr. Fiaschetti restarts me on Seroquel "for insomnia." and adds Topamax, both of which had already been prescribed to me a year prior by Dr. Morano.

Dr. Fiaschetti's notes clearly record that I stopped Topamax because it gave me memory problems and made me dizzy. She disregards this, as well as the adverse reaction I'd had prior with Seroquel. She adds a new one: Trileptal. This makes for an interesting cocktail as each one these medications has a black box warning for causing increased suicidality. The third drug is the charm. (See Appendices I, F, Q, O.)

The Text

I am prepping for my Friday night when I receive the text that shifts my view on Jaxx and subsequently the entire world. It is one of those moments when the information presented is so beyond anything you would ever surmise about your reality that you disregard it as funny because it couldn't possibly be true, or so you tell yourself.

And then more information is presented and slowly your arguments against said information are waning. You begin to raise your tone, furrow your brow and then finally second-guess all that you know is true.

And then,

IT happens.

You imagine the information you've been given is fact. And the very moment you allow for this to be the case, reality looks like something out of a horror film. Nothing is comparable; there is no metaphor, no song lyric, nothing. Mostly the image of yourself frantically looking through an endless room full of mirrors, all different shapes, and sizes to find they aren't even mirrors at all as you get closer, just glass.

So you run, and you run, and you run, and the room just expands for minutes and then hours pass, and you begin to drop visions of this new reality into your mind.

The pieces begin to fall from the sky of intelligence that is your mind and you are faced with an all too likely reality. This is when the decision has to be made.

You either accept what is—the thing that just sixty-minutes prior was not--or you suffocate under the weight of clambering around in that room full of fake mirrors, desperately trying to construct something whose pieces have been partly mixed up and partially thrown out. The simple pieces to your usually logical jigsaw puzzle of life now do not fit the empty spaces that are beginning to freeze out your home.

There are holes in the foundation now. What to do?

That's what happened when Kenna, a friend from Coastal View Elementary and Terpsichore, texted me regarding Oxycontin. The word Oxy is synonymous with a friend's death and another acquaintance's post-overdose state. It is a bad word, one that is not used. It does not exist in my life otherwise until this afternoon. Oxy is this thing that punk rock celebrities overdosed on; of course, I wasn't doing it. How do you even do Oxy? I wondered, envisioning some tinfoil-pipe thing that I'd seen in the movies and then alternatively a syringe and one of those belts tied around Johnny's Cash's arm in *Walk the Line*.

Kenna: Kali- you are a straight-A student, a great dancer, and an amazing person. I've known you and your family forever. I'm telling you this as a friend. I love you. You need to stop doing Oxy. It will kill you.

Me: There's no way I would do that stuff. Why would you say that?

Kenna: I'm not mad, just worried about you. Please tell me if I can help. Please, Kali, stop it now, while you can

Me: I'm serious I have no idea what you are talking about...

Kenna: I know for sure that Jaxx knows what I'm talking about. End it with him, Kali. This isn't healthy anymore; you've got to take care of yourself.

Me: What are you saying??? CALL ME NOW.

"Kali, you don't have to lie," Kenna says in a shaky tone. I pull the phone from my ear to scrunch my eyebrows together in disgust before listening again. I can hear the anger in the back of her throat. She is Jakob's best friend. I know now that this is where the anger was coming from.

"I just..." she sighs, "don't do this to yourself. "She is entirely convinced I am doing Oxy. "I know Jaxx knows exactly what I'm talking about, and I want you to tell him to go to hell for me. Jakob was a good kid before this. And now, all he wants to do is get fucked up on the drug that nearly killed a good friend of mine just months ago. I mean Riley just got out of a coma....I can't believe Jaxx doesn't think about that...you know what, actually, I can. Jaxx doesn't think about anyone, EVER," Kenna says.

Jakob is Jaxx's relatively new best friend. The two of them had been acquaintances forever, and then, quite recently, became inseparable. To check my sources, I give Jakob a call.

I never talked to Jakob outside of math class other than a couple words in a movie theater once. And I never spoke to anyone about that night. So, it is a very surprised "Hello?" on the other end of the call.

I tell Jakob what Kenna said to me and repeat it to him as a fact, adding a request to "Stop, now, please."

His response seals the deal.

"Okay, I'm sorry Kali...I—you know Jaxx is a great guy and I--We didn't want--He didn't want to lie to you and it's not something we started on purpose.."

"Don't apologize to me for that," I say, remembering the behavior he should be apologizing to me about.

I knew Jakob from my fifth-period math class. He was a year above me but he hung out with the Jayden crew from time to time. He isn't one of the regulars, but I grew to enjoy him as a friend in math class. And, I valued the fact that, since he is close to Derrick, he never hit on me. We were just math friends.

A big group of us are at the local outdoor mall. Every Friday the eighth and ninth graders get dropped off at the movie theater there.

We had been drinking this particular Friday. Unfortunately, I am wearing a denim skirt and unfortunately, Jakob is there.

I wake up passed out on Jakob's lap. I am immediately confused as to why I am even with him at all. Before I can lift my head from his chest, I realize he has his hand stuck down my denim skirt. I freeze. I don't want to move. I am utterly confused and mortified as to why he is touching me.

But, I am in the front row of the movie theater. There are drunk members of the class above mine all around me, filling the seats both in our aisle and the rows behind me; there is nowhere to go and I don't want to cause a scene.

He has his sweatshirt over my skirt. I bury my drunk face into Jakob's jacket, pretending he is someone else, and whisper, "Please stop doing that."

I mourned the image I had painted of the kind boy in my fifth-period calculus class. I felt like screaming and crying all at the same time.

You were supposed to be my friend!
HE WAS MY FRIEND!
I black out again. (See Appendix C.)

I woke up to watch the octopus in *Pirates of the Caribbean II* attack a ship. I never re-watched that film. I never will. And I never forgot the taste of green apple Bacardi in the back of my throat, and the hot hand before my vision blurred again.

I never spoke a word of that night. And I didn't speak to him in class anymore, or at all, except in large social gatherings so at not to be asked why. It would be too random for me to hate a friend of a friend.

The hand is dealt.
And Jaxx is calling me.

Meanwhile, my heart is shattering into a million little pieces as I realize that the place I thought I lived is merely a construct of an impossibly perfect world where Jaxx and I told each other everything. It is a complete lie.

I quickly shuffle through the variety of times I'd asked him the question twice, "You swear you are only doing pills?" I'd be staring into a glassy-eyed, slurry Jaxx: the part of him I didn't trust; the part of him I knew would say whatever. He didn't have anything to lose except for me, and he wasn't about to lose that too.

A Letter to the Lost

September 30, 2008

Nighttime falls and the pain pulses so much stronger.
Alone here I wonder if this emptiness will cease.
You left me waiting on the steps where you crushed me.
You've left me torn, longing,
I can't wait for you any longer.

Remembering the fresh, novel days of your charm.
I'd looked you in those dreamy eyes and told you not to lie.
Forgave you like a fool when you deceived me once more.
Your grasp was so protective, so warm.
And your smile,
impossible to disarm.

I cannot say I didn't see the devastation before it occurred;
The train crash phone call transferring over the line.
You'd always said you kept things from me to protect me.
But who were you really protecting?
You. Is what I heard.

What hurts the worst is different that what many envision.
It's a stab to the chest to learn the truth from a friend,
the lies from a lover.
I had really wished you'd grown to become both.
Now all I feel is a deep incision.

Though I'm more proud than ever that you made this choice,
the past will not be erased.
Unexplainable joy will exude from my body if you come back alive.
And by alive, I mean changed.
But I didn't fall in love with changed,
I fell in love with you as you.
And I feel this is lost.

Will we ever be the same?

Kali Rae Wheeler

Will we ever dance
Again
Smile
Laugh
Sincerely?

First Real Attempt

I promised my parents I wouldn't drink at the Homecoming after party.

They learned that I was drinking, called me to check in (I lied and said I was fine) and the story goes that my mother came to pick me up. I didn't answer my phone. Upon receiving my mother's stern text message, I got a fire in my belly to get as drunk as I could in the less than ten minutes it would take my mom to drive from our house to the gated community where the party is located. I manage to pound twenty beers before my mom arrives.

Angrily, heels in hand, I meander down the driveway away from the drunken laughter and smell of cigarettes, beer, and cologne and toward my mother's BMW. I give my mom the silent treatment the entire way home. I neglect even to move a muscle when she asks how the dance went, how my date looked and if I am okay. I maintain my gaze locked on the middle of the dark street. I watch it unravel under the headlights of my mom's car. It becomes blurry and then clears again. I continually blink away the drunkenness that is beginning to fall heavily on me now. By the time we are home, I am drunk. No arguing that. But, I know how to handle myself pretty well by this point. I follow my mother in through the door in the garage to our home. The dog runs over to greet us, and I stumble into the wall.

"Did you drink Kali?" my mom asks, almost taunting me. She knows the answer.

"No, I had like one beer," I lie.

"We told you that you weren't allowed to drink," she says.

"Well someone spilled vodka in my mouth," I say.

A confused-looking father is now standing in the doorway of the office, the room that leads to the garage. He's come to accompany my mother.

"Kali??" My dad says.

"Someone spilled it into my mouth," I repeat.

That was just the beginning of the night. The rest is detailed in my journal, the words becoming messier and messier until they trail off the page.

    I still remember the feeling.

    I was certain I was going to kill myself.

    It all fell into place that night.

October 08, 2008

Well, I wanted to kill myself tonight. I had twenty Seroquel sitting in my sweating palm, but my father barged in on me. So actually, I'm glad I found the whiskey. It's sad that I'd forgotten how much I used to love this stuff. Alcohol solves everything. Honestly, though I'm a joke, I'm a little glad I didn't kill myself, although I can't really write anymore. I must be getting drunker. Shit. Jaxx isn't as good as Blaise was at talking me out of suicide attempts, by the way. I'm way too skinny now, I guess. People are talking. Maybe I don't know. (See Appendices F, O, Q.)
    XO Kali Rae

Dr. Jane M.D. (GP): October 10, 2008
Medication: Synthroid, Ritalin, Trileptal, diazepam, Seroquel
O: 17-year-old urgent stomach pain when she eats since July, headache, ear discomfort, positive bladder infection
A/P: Rx Omnicef for sinus infection

The Thirteenth Stepper

After my father walks in on the Seroquel laden suicide attempt, I need to show my parents a better side of me. It is fall of my Senior Year, and I can't seem to find where I am going or where I came from. All I feel is wrong. I feel guilty for feeling guilty, and I have nowhere to place any of the emotions or any perspective. I just feel bad, really, really bad, sometimes worse, but always bad.

To feel I was doing something right, one Friday night, I search the Internet for AA meetings in my area. Going to a meeting may bring my parents peace of mind. It gave my thoughts an alibi. It gave me an alibi. It gave me control over my emotions by letting me place blame on a disease that was beyond my control.

I feel comfortable looking around the familiar room. There are hundreds of rooms like this in the church, but I recognize this one. The familiarity cradles me like a smell from my childhood that I can't seem to figure out. I went to Sunday school here, where the animal crackers were so tasty, I'd searched for them ever since. I knew the pastor of the church and his family. And this is where Small Groups met, in the building just across the central patio.

This is the same parking lot that Mrs. Bay took us, hung-over teenagers after she'd rounded us all up as the designated driver over the weekend. She'd dump us here to repent.

This is where I was baptized in my Beatles T-shirt with my closest friends who had grown up in this same town.

I am immersed in the meeting. And for the first time in a while, I feel less guilty. I am doing something right. Being here feels right.

There are books laid out and chips given. It's a small meeting, around sixteen people. At the time, I was unaware that these meetings can be ninety people deep.

I effortlessly share my story, clinging to my journal. I don't care who is in the room. This is real, and I need to release it. I notice that I'm the only person without a *Big Book*. In addition to my age, this makes me feel like an outsider. Everyone is at least thirty years older than me. I feel as if each of their tired eyes is glaring at my youth, screaming that it is, "just a phase. You haven't hit rock bottom yet." Assuring me that I should come back when I've hit rock bottom.

Here is the deal, guys, I'd like to prevent that from happening. Hence, the reason I'm sitting with you here on a Friday evening. I don't want to hit "more" of a rock bottom. Because even under the supportive umbrella of my wealthy family, I'd hit my personal lowest point.

Do I need to explain my overall suffering level more?

Is trying to kill myself via Seroquel and a bottle of Wellbutrin samples enough for you?

Is that low enough for acceptance??

Furthermore, my father walked in on this. My dad walked in on his precious youngest daughter, cross-legged on the floor of her bedroom, just as she was after Halloween Night trick-or-treating in her horse costume. However, instead of candies, I was counting pills out. Scissors open next to my knees, ready to slit my wrist if the elixir didn't stop my heart fast enough.

I receive my twenty-four-hour chip and sit through the entire, seemed like ten-hour, meeting. I even read from my neighbor's *Big Book* before the meeting finally ends.

They thank me graciously for being a newcomer. I am told to find a sponsor right away. We get up to leave and a kind-looking gentleman, probably my father's age, approaches me.

"Hi, I'm Greg. Welcome," he says. "I sell the literature, but you're welcome to take a *Big Book* for free."

"Oh, Awesome! Thanks so much!" I grab one off the table. "I'm Kali."

"You look like my daughter. Are you a dancer?" he says.

I am immediately comforted that he has a daughter. He is just a nice guy. He is a dad!

"Yes! How did you know?"

"Your body, the way you look," he says as he look me up and down. "You're so beautiful. I could tell immediately. You're brave to come here. I respect you for that, being so young and all. How old are you?"

I notice most of the people have filed out and get a little nervous. It's just me, this new friend and a group of three ladies by the door.

But, they are lingering.

"I'd love to sponsor you. I think I could help. Your story is very relatable, and I think we would get along great," he says.

I start feeling creepy inside as he brings his hand up to cup the outside of my arm.

"Hi Kali, how are you," the ladies had approached! "We aren't supposed to have co-ed sponsors. I think Kali is just fine with us. Thanks, Greg."

"Oh!" Greg jumps back like he has no idea someone would be looking out for me. He's surprised. The group of ladies surrounds me without saying a word. I am protected.

"Thank you for bringing the literature, Greg. Come on Kali; we'll walk you out," the woman says.

At each following meeting, Greg sits next to me, brings me gifts, and creeps me out to the point that I quit attending meetings altogether. Thanks for the book, Greg, and for forever tainting the wonderful culture Bill W. created.

Translation: Fuck you, Greg.

Dr. Fiaschetti M.D. (psychiatrist): October 17, 2008
Discontinued Topamax due to memory problems and kidney stones
Lithium Carbonate 200mg in AM and 600mg at bedtime

The Gift That Keeps on Giving: Topamax's Kidney Stones

I have been suffering from flank pain for months. After rounds of antibiotics and several other tests, I finally get a scan of my kidneys. Once again, Dr. Jane misses something big. There are more than a dozen stones in my kidneys. Dr. Scott calls us with the news and the instructions to stop taking Topamax immediately and to rest while this process continues to run its course.

Along with the stones are the tests that accompanied them—aka being strapped down to a hospital table that harnesses you onto it like The Vitruvian Man. When the technician leaves the room, after inserting a catheter, which is just about the most painful thing I've ever experienced, they flip a switch; the bed lifts itself to a standing position. Now you're like a squirrel that's run into a glass window. You're sprawled out. And, when the beeping sounds and mechanical arms creak around the plastic equipment. You're alone, of course. The scariest tests and procedures always require this. And, there were the handful of late-night Emergency Room visits to calm the fever and pain medications to dampen the excruciating pain that accompanied their removal. (See Appendix Q.)

In a study to find if Topamax directly causes kidney stone formation, the conclusion is simple:

"Treatment with topiramate causes systemic metabolic acidosis, markedly lower urinary citrate excretion, and increased urinary pH. These changes increase the propensity to form calcium phosphate stones" (Welch 2006).

Dr. Scott M.D. (GP): November 03, 2008
Chief Complaint: UTI and flank pain
O: Multiple kidney stones

Dr. Scott M.D. (GP): November 06, 2008
Chief Complaint: Flank pain
A/P: Rx Flomax & Rx Ibuprofen 800, F/U next week

Dr. Scott M.D. (GP): November 10, 2008
Medications: Synthroid, Vicodin didn't help much
S: Kidney Stones
A/P: Emergency Room Now

Dr. Scott M.D. (GP): November 12, 2008
Medications: Synthroid, Cipro and feeling depressed
S: F/U ER visit 11/10, a dozen kidney stones, appetite is back
A/P: Rx Macrobid for 6 months

Dr. Scott M.D. (GP): December 10, 2008
Medications: Synthroid, Trileptal, Topamax stopped
S: 100 temp. for 3 days. 4 kidney stones passed
A/P: Norco ordered, Vicodin doesn't help, called in Cipro

A Trip to Arrowhead
Turns into a Trip to See Cathy

It's a little over a year since Jaxx, and I got together, and we are still inseparable. We do everything together. Jaxx and I just arrived at the snowy paradise of his Arrowhead cabin. We would have the entire six bedrooms, pool table, grand piano, full kitchen with garage and cars, to ourselves for a week. We are super excited. After we get settled in the master bedroom on the second story, Jaxx pulls out the baggie of Norco. The plan is to ration out the Norco. We have a full bottle of pills when we arrive at Jaxx's Lake Arrowhead cabin. Jaxx, like always, had control of them. He counted out twenty oblong yellow pills and slid them over to me.

"We don't have very many more," Jaxx cautions.

"K."

I pop three in my mouth and chew; the nausea ceases.

Jaxx taught me the "chewing them" trick on day one. It takes the coating off and allows for the chemicals to absorb quicker. The downside is the sour, yellow gunk left in your teeth and its horrible taste.

He would mix them in a bottle of Fiji. Watching him pop them in gave me a rush of calm. I knew I'd be floating soon. The water slowly turned a hazy, light yellow. The graininess of the last sip was always the best part unless I'd taken too many, and then it would make me vomit.

I grew into a habit of watching Jaxx and the Norco each day. I never got any on my own, but I saw Jaxx, literally, every, single day. And every, single day, Jaxx brought pills.

I had had knee surgery a few months prior and was struggling with kidney stones as well as all the dancer-related issues that came with rehearsing and choreographing full out without a proper warm-up.

Jaxx knew how much pain I was in physically because he had back issues of his own from a drunk-driving accident.

The first few days in Arrowhead were a dream. We had an entire seven-bedroom cabin to ourselves, a very beautiful boat that Jaxx could drive, our dock, any money we needed, a pool table, California king-sized bed, grand piano...should I continue? We had everything. It was perfect. Oh! And there was snow!

And then the house started caving in on us both.

We'd rationed the Norco out for a few days and knew we'd need more at some point. I never paid attention to any of the logistics of it. But I did know that he kept double for himself and hid them. If he didn't, he would figure out a way to con more.

His mother was the person who gave him his first Norco. When I was dealing with kidney stone pain, she gave him an emergency supply to give me. I had already been taking Norco with him, but that was the first time his mother was directly involved. She was the sweetest, but she was a mess.

"I'm going to go to the ER," Jaxx says.

"What will you say?" I ask.

"I don't know. Just wait here. I'll be back," he locks the door behind him and drives into the snowy evening.

About an hour later, I get a text:

Jaxx: Fuck this place, I'm coming back.

I can tell by the way he soberly enters the cabin, that he has been unsuccessful. His ER bracelet clutches his wrist like a "Livestrong" band. He is too sick to remove it. I can tell he is hurting, and I am too.

30 minutes later:

"I can break my arm. I can totally break my arm," I say.

I am dying to get more. The trip was fantastic, and now I feel like I have the flu, mixed with a terrible head cold.

"Look, you can just hit it while I hold it out this way." I demonstrate.

"No way, don't be stupid," he says un-amused, but I am totally not kidding.

He grabs a knife. "I could just cut myself," he says slowly.

I snatch the butcher's knife away from him.

"Do NOT cut yourself Jaxx. I can break a finger or something, look..."

"Kali! Stop!! Just trust me. Let's lie down. I'll call Stephen," he says.

As the hours pass, I get worse and worse. The comedown from opiates is something I wouldn't wish on anyone. If we had had to come off of benzos at the same time, it would have been more than a mess. Neither one of us would have been able to move.

Good thing we had a surplus of Somas and Xanax, they don't touch the symptoms of opiate withdrawal. The pain in my muscles was sickening, and my head throbbed like I'd smacked into a mogul on a Black Diamond slope in Mammoth.

We've been lying on the couch, staring at the fireplace in the living room for a full day now. Jaxx is on and off the phone with a handful of different people, explaining that he was in Arrowhead, and that he needs a favor and then saying;

"Fuck, bro!"

I swear I heard that phrase over thirty times that afternoon.

After the last phone call, he sits down next to my feverish self, laid out on the sofa like a sick child. He sits, folded over, head in hands.

"Fuuuuucccck, Kali, I'm dying," Jaxx says.

I push myself up from the cushions. The wooziness is overwhelming. I steady myself with two feet on the Persian rug, before I can comb my fingers through his perfectly straightened hair. Yes, he had a mini-straightener, and yes, he straightened his faux-hawk every day.

Jaxx was about six foot two, a hundred and sixty pounds, athletic when he played football, but since his accident had been prone to losing massive amounts of weight depending on where he was in his addiction cycle. When he was really thin, it was confusing, because he was still so good-looking; Jonathan Rhys Meyers is who he got most of the time.

But, when you looked at him, you would realize his True Religion jeans had to be only the equivalent of a woman's 28, and they were falling off his hips. His head looked bigger and bigger as his eyes sank further and further. He looked like a skeleton boy, at one point, a skeleton boy but with perfect hair in a sports coat. When things got really bad, he wasn't awake enough to straighten his hair.

He looked pretty good right now, but he wasn't.

Cathy is Jaxx's special doctor. He kept her number on a post-it, and people paid him for the info. I never understood why it was such a gift to have this woman's phone number, but he kept her number guarded like he was guarding the Holy Grail. Although the photographs say differently, we were both very ill.

After a day filled with phone calls on Jaxx's end, and napping on and off for me, Jaxx grabbed me by the shoulders, sitting me up, and almost shaking me, he is so excited:

"Get dressed; we're going to see Cathy."

"Wait, isn't she in the middle of nowhere?"

"Yes, we are taking a road trip. She said she could get me in today."

"So everything is figured out?" I ask; I never knew how the pills got to him or how or even if he paid for them. They always just showed up in my hand when I had a headache.

Once you start taking opiates, you feel more pain. It's an interesting dichotomy, and I wonder if this is somehow manipulated on purpose to gain addicts. You don't know that the drugs are firing the pain signals in your brain. You feel great at the moment, but very shortly after, you start hurting again, whether it's a migraine or a neck ache or a stomachache, your nerves fire like they are being injured.

And on top of that, once you start taking them, even for a small amount of time, the withdrawal is worse than anything I could have imagined. And, it's the only addiction that is never let go by your brain. No matter what, your brain will recognize the familiar sensation and jump right back on the bandwagon to destruction.

I always said they were called painkillers because they refused to let you feel your emotions that they had nothing to do with physical pain.

Jaxx forces me to get out of bed: moaning and everything. He wants me to accompany his, just-as-sick self to breakfast via boat (yacht).

"I don't care, Kali. You need to eat," Jaxx says. The hangover is apparent in his tone and paleness.

"No, Jaxx. I will puke on your dash."

"Great, put this on. We're taking the boat. I want to show you my favorite restaurant."

He throws me one of my favorite things on the planet, his cashmere Burberry sweater, the one with the sleeves that are too long in a perfect sort of way.

I look down at his super soft, white V-neck, I'd slept in, and realize that all of my favorite things are his. There is a bundled-up American Apparel button-up sweater bunched up on my pillow: the burgundy one.

I loved his clothes.

I make it through breakfast. The restaurant is charming. It's right on the lake. I can tell Jaxx feels awful, but he maintains his "in charge" strut. I struggle to make it up the dock to the driveway where the Jeep is parked. Before I know what hit me, I am swept off my feet, and placed in the passenger seat.

"Jaxx Alexander Moreau..." I whine, "You don't have to be so cute."

"I can't help it."

He smiles from the driver's seat like a stuck-up Lacrosse player and then morphs into crossing his eyes and curling his lips.

"Ah! No! Stop!" I laugh.

"Let's DO THIS." His voice is funny, like a high school football coach.

Driving down the mountain, Jaxx grabs my hand, and I swoon into him in the beat-up Jeep. It is the only thing he owns that isn't brand new. The Jeep was his car. Although, while in Newport, we spent the majority of the time driving his mother's new S-Class Mercedes-Benz, I liked the Jeep. It reminded me that we were still just a high school couple, with simple problems, problems like figuring out how we would move to LA separately but at the same time.

Although I feel super nauseated and exhausted, (thanks, opiates), looking over at Jaxx, I know that the pain will be gone soon. I feel a tinge of adrenaline mixed with a fluttery heart.

He is just so damn dreamy.

He was an Edward...definitely.

Even as our car slid out from under us, due to the snowy roads, he stayed calm and collected. I was screaming, and he was telling me it was going to be okay.

"Relax!" he says, reaching over the console to grab my thigh and secure me to the seat. I didn't stop screaming. By the time the car stopped on the deserted street we were traveling down to the local market, Jaxx is almost in tears laughing at me. My mother called at just the right time.

"Yeah, one second," Jaxx says, laughing and puts my mother on speaker phone.

"Mom!" I shout.

"Kali! I heard you are quite the dramatic ski buddy! Relax, Pumpkin; that's why you have chains on the car. Cars slide on ice," she says.

"I thought I was going to die!"

Jaxx and my mom laugh in unison. My mother never acts like this. I'm surprised she's calm. She's never calm. I like it.

I wake up to the Jeep stopping and pull my head off of the doorframe; Jaxx's hand is still lodged between my thighs. This simple gesture always made me feel safe, no matter what.

"Good morning, babe!" he says cheerfully. "I'm going to give you the keys. It shouldn't take long."

"Like an hour?"

"No less than that. Just don't leave the car," he warns. "It's not safe. Text me if you need anything.

The scenery is bleak. We are in the middle of the state; I'm guessing. We are in the parking lot of, what looks like one of those sketchy malls. I watch him walk away and felt a surge of gratitude. We would feel better soon.

I wake up an hour later to the sound of two male voices.

No Jaxx.

The two men are getting into the car next to ours. They look unkempt and thin. Their baseball caps and denim frighten me.

I play the mix we burned together for the drive to Arrowhead to calm myself. It's been an hour since Jaxx left, and still no Jaxx.

But, I am so used to waiting an hour and a half past Jaxx's said arrival time that I planned to wait.

It has been over two hours now, and no text, nothing.

I begin calling him frantically. I don't know who this doctor is or how it works; maybe it was a drug deal. I start panicking, remembering the scary men who parked right next to the Jaxx's truck. The gray afternoon isn't helping the mood of it all.

Finally, I see him walking to the car with two slips of paper in his hand and a glazed look on his face. He was feeling it.

"Sorry it took forever, there were like fifteen new patients."

"Fifteen?" I say.

"Yeah, someone must have gotten her info and sold it like an idiot," he says, "fucking idiot."

After calling around to every pharmacy within a thirty-mile radius, he finds a Target about twenty minutes away that has the goods. He needs Brand-name because "the generic shit is bullshit," he says. And we need an enormous quantity.

The scavenger hunt is not over yet.

Once at Target, we need the pharmacy to fill all three drugs at once, in the huge amount and somehow go around insurance without asking questions.

I feel like a criminal walking around Target. I'm nervous. I feel like I am doing something wrong.

I'm nervous they won't fill the script.

I pace around the entire store probably six times.

I watch from the Band-Aid aisle as he whips out his money clip and hands the pharmacist several bills. One or two of those were probably hundred dollar bills. He liked to carry those around, and he had told me once that people buy the drugs he had for eighty dollars per pill, depending on the strength. One Xanax bar was ten dollars to buy from someone on the street. Somas were the cheap ones, like ten dollars for twenty at times.

"Yew!" he shouts as we exit the store, "Let's get back up the mountain!" He pulls me to him and kisses me on the head, squeezing me like a doll. "BAAABE! You're the cutest thing I've ever seen. Let's go home."

I must have resembled Puss in Boots staring back at him and the bag holding two hundred Norco, three hundred Somas and two hundred and fifty Xanax bars.

Uneven Ground: The Leather Journal

January 07, 2009

I haven't taken Trileptal or Lithobid for like a day or two now. I wasn't sure which one was making me feel sick, but I just felt weird, and I still do. Like I keep missing keys and having to go back and retype things. Also, I can't write at all it's weird. I feel disconnected from my body, like drunk all the time but emotionless and not happy. I can't drive at all because I am so nervous about crashing because everything just seems distorted.

My reflexes are slow, and things seem closer or farther than they are. I have blurred vision, and it feels like I'm looking through goggles all the time. Like I have no peripheral vision. I am shaky and just overall uncomfortable. Way more than dizzy. It feels like I can't walk, and when I do walk it's like I'm walking on uneven ground. Like on a boat or something. It hurts my head to look around and try to sort things out…I'm not even kidding. My hands seem super weird like I can't feel things correctly and they feel swollen and are hard to move. I have cold sweats all the time, and I forget what I'm saying in the middle of conversations. Sometimes I have to stop and laugh and ask what we were talking about.

Honestly, I feel like I just need to lie in bed and wait for this "flu" to pass. I'm incredibly weak, and it takes a lot out of me to move in this kind of state. I cannot wait for this to pass. I wake up each morning and look at the clock until it is around four and then get excited for nighttime to come. What a life. I really can't get anything done, and I feel worthless. I have so much on my plate, and I just can't handle it while being this ill.

I need to go to physical therapy for my knee so that I can dance again, but I've also had kidney stones and interstitial cystitis for a while. Every day is challenging, and it's getting worse it seems. I've lost all my passion for music and writing and working with Marcus. I don't want to be around people because I feel awkward and I've never felt awkward around people like ever. It has to be these fucked up meds that I'm on. Right now I can't drive, can't work with Marcus, can't write, can't exercise, can't enjoy myself, can't hang out with friends normally and don't want to, can't communicate like a normal person. (See Appendices O, P.) XO Kali Rae

Dr. Scott M.D. (GP): January 12, 2009
S: Nausea and vomiting, blood in vomit (See Appendix P.)
A/P: Told to go to ER right away

Dr. Fiaschetti M.D. (psychiatrist): February 22, 2009
Xanax RX 1mg replaced Valium, which may have worsened interstitial cystitis, preferred Valium but it didn't work the same the second time

Waiting for the Suboxone Delivery

By February, I am juggling a full high school senior year as well as an insane amount of college course at the local community college. I talked Jaxx into starting school again with me for the spring, and he agreed, although he wasn't able to hold onto his spot in the Freshman English course. He never took any of the classes that I did. And he would regularly, without even the slightest thought, just decide not to go to class anymore. It made me crazy.

By March of 2009, I decide I need space.

I didn't know what I was feeling anymore. The relationship had become so intertwined with this sick codependent by nature, addiction. I never had to buy my drugs. He was always my only supplier. I didn't know if what I was feeling was a love of the drugs or real feelings for Jaxx. I was becoming incredibly laden with guilt and disgusted by the whole thing. Could these drugs have tricked me? Could I have just fallen in love with the feeling g of being high with this person? The relationship had become engrossed in the constant drug use. And Jaxx was looking worse and worse, paler and more ghostly. As he did when I first met him, and he had to go to court in the morning, completely out of his mind messed-up.

He came over that day when I told him and carefully divided up the Suboxone that his doctor had given him. Not really by coincidence, but a necessity, we both had separately decided we needed to stop taking opiates. Jaxx had the luxury of being honest with his mother about things, and so he had been given a medicine called Subutex to wean him off of the opiates, He generously shared them with me, even rationed them out when I said I need a break o get my head together. He left them in a little baggie in my desk drawer and made sure I knew that I could call if I needed more: that this was separate from our relationship. (See Appendix S.)

The Debutante Ball

It's June of my Senior Year. I am a part of a community service program and the annual debutante ball is this month, and I need Jaxx to be my date. I'd be accepting my award for the hours of community service I'd worked over the past four years, and we are doing a fashion show that requires multiple costume changes and a male date for the men's clothes. Jaxx and I are together, hesitantly. He has not been doing good lately. But he has been going up to Los Angeles a lot lately, and he had just been scouted for a highly regarded talent agency. Modeling was his thing.

"I signed you up to model with me...because you're my date, it kind of comes with that..." I say to Jaxx.

"Cool," Jaxx says.

"I think they're just going to have the guys wear white tees and 7 Jeans," I say.

"Fuck 7 Jeans. Is Jayden coming?" Jaxx asks.

Heidi is a very active member of the Charity League, and Jayden was dating Heidi.

"Yeah, she's president," I respond.

"I'm down. I was just talking to that agency that scouted me at Fashion Island. They want me to go up to LA next week. I think I'm staying with Stephen," Jaxx says.

"What, that's amazing! Good job, babe! You'll be here in time for Saturday though, right? It's kind of one of those, RSVP and need to be there on time things..." (Jaxx was typically an hour and a half late on a good day).

"Ya," Jaxx replies.

"Jaxx, you really can't smoke at this thing. Please, babe?"

Jaxx is leaning on one of the pillars outside one of our favorite spots, The Bay Club. Tonight it's the location of the Charity League Fashion Show and Senior Banquet.

This is where the members receive recognition for the four years, and many hours of community service performed. There's also a fashion show tonight. We will model several outfits from local boutiques after changing out of our mandatory white dresses: the ones that had to be pre-approved by the head of the organization, which was, difficult, to say the least.

"I'm serious. It's like the most Newport-y thing of all things you could go to," I add, watching Jaxx as he pulls me in closer to him so that I have to tilt my head up to speak to him.

"BAAABE," he moans, pulling me into him, "come on. I won't smoke at your Dilettante Ball—"

"Charity League Fashion Show," I cut him off, "I wouldn't do a Dilettante Ball. Are you kidding?" I look up at him shocked. "They are also honoring me because I did a thousand hours of community service and started the book drive annnnnnnd the shirt company aaaaannnnd..."

"I know, Babe. Because you are the smartest, most beautiful, kindest, most stressed-out..."

"Hey!"

"Babe, relax. You're beautiful. I won't smoke at your party."

He reaches into his True Religions to answer a call, throwing the butt of the cigarette on the pavement next to the valet stand. He taps it with his bright white Jack Purcells to put it out. He looks at me coyly as he bends down to pick it up and throw it in the trash can left out from trash day.

His cigarette butts started to litter the gutter of our Newport Coast home. My mother began to leave empty coffee containers out next to the wooden bench in front of the rose bushes, so that our gardener, Manuel, wouldn't have to keep picking them up and piling them by the rocks. It took a lot of convincing to get Jaxx to throw away his cigarette butts.

Seeing Jaxx in front of our pale yellow country French home, was like seeing an Inuit in Arizona. His tall movie star-looking self, smoking a cigarette, dressed impeccably, like he's straight out of a film from the 1930s. My neighbors knew who he was:

"That's Kali's boyfriend!"

They'd wave politely and then gossip.

Under the Lights: Valedictorian Speech

My eyes dart over to the big clock in the back of my Oceanography 101 Lab class, just a few more minutes. "Kali, you can go ahead and get to your graduation," the Professor announces to the class of college kids.

"Thank you!" I say.

My lab partner begins a slow clap. It builds into a full-on rambunctious crowd. The class is whistling, whooping and cheering, over-enthusiastically as I gather my things in a rush. I blush intensely but invisibly, due to my skin coloring.

I am cutting it close. I throw my favorite sequined messenger bag (the one Tessa and Kendall and I had gotten at the swap meet) over my shoulder and run out of the classroom, through the main room of the building and crack open the double doors.

As I run on the freshly laid concrete toward the auditorium on the other side of campus, I swing my bag around to the front of me, pulling out my laminated valedictorian speech.

"Shit," I breathe, as I remember I that I'd forgotten to practice last night. I was busy writing the thesis for the oceanography final.

The Oceanography class required that we predict the nautical charts and weather conditions as well and how they'd affect the specimens we were able to collect on our last day of class. Our quarter culminated in an actual oceanic exploration where we would be pulling up real sea life, including sharks, and separating and reporting on the types of mud we found, the salinity of the water, the temperature, etc. I could go on for hours about it, just really fun stuff.

I reach into my back pocket and take out a little shard of Xanax I'd saved. The blue pill doesn't split in a clean line, the light blue powder showers onto the black fabric of the bag. It was the third time today that I'd done that, and it wasn't even 1 p.m. yet.

Shit. I hope I don't get loopy.

My whole family, minus Kayla, plus Kara, as well as Jaxx and my grandmother, are all dressed up. They are carrying bouquets and looking beautiful: straight out of a sitcom, the perfect family. I immediately feel a sense of accomplishment.

Upon hugging my grandmother, I feel a huge wash of appreciation. She had flown in all the way from New Mexico to be here.

Jaxx is holding a full bouquet of roses. (Gatsby, please!)

Kara has flowers too, and my brother is even dressed up. My dad took off work and wrote me a beautiful card. Everything is perfect.

As I present my speech, I feel no nerves at all. Looking out into the sea of proud parents, I instead feel an obligation to inspire my fellow students. The few fumbles over sentences sting with the reminder that I am indeed under the influence in such a way that I am tripping over my Valedictorian speech.

Epilogue:
My Doctors are Famous

Dr. Cathy on Prime-Time News

F lash forward to 2014.
I traveled down the 405 to see my parents for the weekend. I was making dinner with my mom when an all-too-familiar story flashed across the prime-time news. And, it wasn't a breaking news story; it had been developing for years. The criminal was finally being sentenced.

The story was hauntingly familiar. Even so, I couldn't quite grasp that it was Cathy. I knew, deep down, that it was Cathy, but I'd never met her.

The news spoke of an Asian woman, a doctor, finally charged with murder in the overdose deaths of three individuals from Orange County.

I knew Cathy had an Asian last name because I'd seen it in Jaxx's phone. It was her. I knew it. I could finally put a face to the elusive and deadly women: the reason why so many of my friends were farther down the rabbit hole than ever could have been possible without this crooked doctor. I shivered at the sight of her mug shot. The faceless doctor whom Jaxx traveled so far to see, whose phone number he guarded with his life was staring at me from a terrible mug shot.

The story was all too familiar; the long drive, the awkward office situated in one of those Chinese restaurants and a take-kwon-do studio, the kids who drove hours from Orange County to see her, the three drugs she prescribed in insanely large amounts.

Upon watching the news, I recollected the wash of relief that came over me when Jaxx got back into the car with the three prescriptions, Xanax, Somas, and Norco, and told me it was time to find a pharmacy. I was dumbfounded by the sheer amount of pills once the prescriptions are filled. Jaxx would sell most of them to make up for the cost of the visit and still have about a bag of each pill left. At the time, I felt relief mostly, but also confusion as to how this was ever legal. How could someone be this backward as to prescribe this many pills and in this combination? It was deplorable, to say the least. And now I know that in many cases, it turned deadly.

Dr. Morano Close Behind

As soon as I saw Cathy on the News, I knew I had to find Dr. Morano.

I ran to the computer to type in his name, and the results were more validating than ever. They were terrible, yes, but they provided the fire I needed to continue on this path to figure out what went wrong in my treatment with so many of these crooked doctors and to stop others from having to go through the same hell.

When I searched Dr. Morano's name on the Internet, I tried not to be surprised by the articles that so perfectly lined up with everything I remembered about his strange and reckless behavior. Not only did he show up in conjunction with Cathy (the absorbent amount of Norco, Xanax, and Soma's doctor) Dr. Morano was clinically nuts. Like my mother had guessed, Dr. Morano had a mental break. He had been tased in his own backyard, admitted to a mental institution for a month. This is when he lost his pristine office space and explains why the office was boarded up that day. Dr. Morano had been treating his own bipolar disorder with the Seroquel samples. There were even several instances where the authors refer to his Hawaiian shirts and the samples he gave out like Halloween candy.

The part that hurts are the deaths that came about due to his negligence. Dr. Morano has little more than a couple of suspensions from practicing, yet he's played a key role in several cases of manslaughter, ranging from overdose deaths to vehicular manslaughter. There are many accounts of his inaccurate notes and terrible record keeping. And it's been brought to the attention of the medical board that he didn't check his records before prescribing drugs that interacted with one another, AND he didn't properly write down the medications he had prescribed.

Truly, the fact is stranger than fiction.

I often wondered how I happened to be right in the middle of all of this. The answer is that I wasn't the only one, far from it. And many people suffered, some fatally after coming into contact with this physician.

I also found that Dr. Morano is still operating out of that weird office in the middle of nowhere: the desolate building where he kept his samples of prescriptions in a set of plastic drawers next to him. The building I remember so well from that last appointment.

Retrieving the Medical Records

In 2014, I gave Dr. Morano a call to get my medical records. It turned into quite the task. I thought it ended when I finally received the manila envelope, but I was wrong, and $80 poorer.

The records were gibberish, except for one, typed-out, in May of 2007. Most of the papers had a couple of words scribbled across the neatly lined pages. No dates were recorded and most of the time nothing is even written under "Medications." I sorted through the payment receipts to find the dates of the actual visits.

I scheduled an appointment via phone with Dr. Morano just to have him translate his writing to me. His voice was, just as I had remembered: frenzied and all too sure of himself.

It became evident, a few minutes into the call, that he was giving me the same sentences over and over: that Dr. Morano is making up answers on the spot. He kept repeating the same three medications, forgetting to mention the handful of different samples he gave me at various times. He had a tendency to withhold information, and instead of answering the question, repeated himself until he hypothesized it into a new idea.

He runs through specific appointment dates by continually summarizing my treatment, circling back to his point of needing to be on an atypical drug. He doesn't disagree or argue when I ask about certain drugs that are not noted on my chart that he'd given to me as samples, (aka almost all of them), he rushes past them, rambling. When I ask him a few times about a certain medication, he'll finally say, "it made you more depressed," or "it gave you headaches, I think, or you were tired, I think an atypical would work for you.'"

It was a disaster. I tried for the first few minutes, and then let him do his thing. By the end, I simply asked him to list the medications he had prescribed and went from there.

I had to ask him about each drug, from memory: For example, Effexor. I didn't need to be refreshed on the brain shivers that Jaxx attempted to medicate with Norco that he got from his mother, but I wanted information from the doctor. I, at least, wanted to make sure he wouldn't deny giving me those medications.

"What about—[insert drug from list below]?"

"It made you more depressed," he pauses, "Yeah, more depressed, not good."

Interesting. That's what the list says under just about every other drug.

His answer, when asked about specific dates, was to sidestep the question.

I say, "What about the appointment in April of 2007 that I see here?"

"Um, let's see, by April...well, let's look here, hmmm, okay, so I think you were taking an atypical, was it lithium, or look here, oh and that was when we—or no, that was when we tried Seroquel, maybe that was—wait, oh yeah that's about in May when we decided to add Topamax..."

Good thing I could cross reference with the other very well recorded doctor's records, as well as journals and parents.

After years of being off any psychotropic drug, and without even asking me how I am, Dr. Morano says that "mood stabilizers would be the only treatment" for me, that "traditional antidepressants didn't work," and that "lithium or Depakote would be a good."

Among the drugs Dr. Morano forgot to note but agreed I was given:

- Effexor—this drug was like coming off of heroin (or what I would imagine).
- Wellbutrin
- Abilify
- Lyrica
- Topamax
- Zoloft—He stated that this "made me more depressed." Dr. Fiaschetti's notes say it made me "highly sexualized."
- Tegretol—He had nothing to say and changed the subject after "made you more depressed."
- Risperdal—this was a sample that my mother quickly disposed of this sample explaining in the car, that it was used for schizophrenia and that there would be no way I was taking it

When I spoke with Dr. Fiaschetti, there is an entirely different tone than Dr. Morano. She is irritated. And although she quickly faxes me over a copy of what is more like a typed-out timeline, she doesn't answer any questions and makes it clear that this is a hassle.

There are no explanations beside increased dosages. Although it looks like an organized record, it is largely empty. The records illustrated the absurdity of the amount of drugs I was tried on and off of in that short period of time. Every month I was on a new medication, and when she ran out of ideas, she would try the same medications Dr. Morano tried.

Mother Knew Best All Along

I argued for years against my mom's point of view. She screamed at times at these physicians who wouldn't allow her to intervene in their diagnoses and subsequent prescriptions. She was sure I wasn't born this way. She knew I was acting differently because of the drugs they had given me in an attempt to classify me as something they understood.

I accused her of trying to take me off of medicines that were helping me.

Doctors diagnosed me with; attention deficit hyperactivity disorder, post-traumatic stress disorder, fibromyalgia, GAD, bipolar disorder, sleep disorder, and depression.

I was painted to fit inside every single category that these people could look up in their book of disorders. It was a messed-up paint by numbers game, but instead, paint-by-encyclopedia of symptoms and their corresponding pill game.

It wasn't her right to tell me that I didn't have a label. After all the struggle to find where I fit, all the time spent trying to figure out why I felt the way that I did, she was trying to re-complicate my life.

I understand now that it'd be hard to watch a child grow from a beam of light into a laser beam of self-sabotaging genius.

Afterword

When I first started diving back into all the places I had hidden deep in the vault that held "the missing years," I had a lot of trouble separating the present from the past. For instance, when a new artist would come into the studio, I would be caught up in the emotions of the past and I wouldn't be able to answer simple questions in the present.

I shut myself up so very tight that everything was a secret. Watching the patterns of the past, I decided that I didn't want to create any more of the persona that was me. I didn't want to leave any trail behind me. I wanted to disappear. Slowly, I have found that hiding isn't fulfilling either and trying to erase every footprint behind you before stepping forward is a complete waste of time.

Becoming smaller does not build anybody else up. And, speaking softer, does not bother people less. Erasing myself from every person and situation does not rewrite history, and hiding not to make a mistake, does not help anybody.

We are all put on this planet to make mistakes, learn, fall, get up, try again, and repeat. We are on a Hero's Journey.

All those years ago, in that leather journal, I promised myself I would never give up and so many times during my life I have stopped a negative pattern of thinking by remembering that I promised I would not give up.

I'd like for you to make a promise to yourself. Once you think of a promise, I need you to write it down somewhere: write it in on the page, write it on your hand, just write it down.

It is only through living that we gain strength to conquer our deepest fears.

Dear Life,
Bring it on.
XO Kali Rae

Appendices

Appendix A

Rx Fx: Ativan (Lorazepam)

Out of all the emotions I brought to the appointment with Dr. Thompson, sadness is the one thing that I absolutely described to her that afternoon. Amazing, because the warnings/precautions label of the drug guide for Ativan says prescribing this drug may not only lead to dependency, but that it could make me more depressed.

> "Preexisting depression may emerge or worsen; not for use with primary depressive disorder or psychosis...May impair mental/physical abilities. Use may lead to physical and psychological dependence...May have abuse potential...possible suicide in patients with depression; do not use in such patients without adequate antidepressant therapy" (PDR 2016).

Also, in a case where my so-called "phobia" does not disrupt anything in my life at all, why would someone prescribe this drug so easily? It is dangerous in adults, and has not even been properly tested for children. It seems that this Dr. had no idea she was playing with fire.

> "Ativan should be used with extreme caution in CHILDREN younger than 12 years old; safety and effectiveness in these children have not been confirmed" (Drugs.com 2016).

Ativan (lorazepam) is part of a group of drugs that are sometimes called skeletal muscle relaxants. They depress the central nervous system (Physicians Desk Reference [PDR] 2016). Ativan is also a sedative, an anti-anxiety medication belonging to the class of benzodiazepines (benzos), a class of drugs that would become all too familiar to me after this.

Ativan is a schedule IV drug. (Medshadow 2016) This category assignment says that Ativan's so-called risk of abuse is low, in comparison to say, Oxycontin, a Schedule II narcotic, or Vicodin, a little bit less addictive as a Schedule III narcotic. Adderall, for instance, is a Schedule II stimulant. Xanax and Valium are both in the same group of schedule IV benzos (Medshadow 2016). In doctor-speak, Ativan is relatively harmless. But, that's far from the truth. In conjunction with other medicines or alcohol, Ativan can produce fatal results:

> "Increased CNS-depressant effects with other CNS depressants (e.g., alcohol, barbiturates, antipsychotics, sedative/hypnotics, anxiolytics, antidepressants, narcotic analgesics, sedative antihistamines, anticonvulsants, anesthetics); may lead to potentiallyfatal respiratory depression" (PDR 2016).

Appendix B

Rx Fx: Soma (Carisoprodol)

The FDA warns that there have been "post-marketing reports of motor vehicle accidents" (Food and Drug Administration [FDA] 2009), due to the use of Soma. They also warn although it is not a controlled substance that Soma not only produces "withdrawal signs, there are published case reports of dependence," but also "elicits barbiturate-like effects" (FDA 2009). And, "in the post-marketing experience with Soma, cases of dependence, withdrawal, and abuse have been reported with prolonged use" (FDA 2009).

Appendix C

Drug-Induced Black Outs

Throughout high school I blacked out. It became inevitable. No matter what I did, if I drank, at some point of the night, I would lose consciousness mentally, yet appear conscious outwardly.

It was like watching a movie where the film play without issue right up until a certain point and then the screen suddenly goes completely black: no picture or sound. You wait and wait for the movie to pick back up where it left off, but instead, the film flickers back for a moment, but the scene is blurry, and the characters are now in a completely different time and place than they had been when the screen turned black. Then, before you can sort out what is going on or how the characters got to this new place and time, the screen goes black once more.

Often I would learn that I did mortifying things. It wasn't that I just *said* embarrassing things, because that is a given drunk person attribute, I would *do* things that normal drunk people would never attempt. I heard from different people at various times that at a certain point in the night (usually coinciding with when my memory goes dark) my eyes changed. They started to look "vacant."

"You weren't looking back at me, you were, but not really," they would try and explain before shaking there heads. "It was weird, it wasn't you. You didn't look the same."

I attributed these blackouts to the amount of liquor I consumed. And since I don't drink at all anymore, I don't really need to find the answer. But, I have strong intuition about this now, because many times people did not believe that I had blacked out because I drank just as much as they did or because "You didn't even drink that much though!" It is very difficult to explain blacking out to a teenager. Most of the time they think you are exaggerating to look cool.

I stumbled across an article about blackouts while researching drug side effects and the definition was spot on for what I experienced countless times.

"A blackout is a period of time where a person is conscious, but is unable to recall any of the events, situations or experiences afterward. A blackout is not passing out, as passing out means you are unconscious. During periods of blackouts, people engage in wild, thoughtless behaviors that they would not typically engage in otherwise" (Newlifeoutlook 2016).

My curiosity, for no specific reason, leads me to search name of the antidepressant I was taking before the first black out of this book, alongside the words: "blackout" and "alcohol."

The results are staggering.

I am entranced. I continue down the list of drugs, searching each drug I had been prescribed next to the word "blackouts." I find numerous blog posts of worried individuals wondering if anyone else experiences blackouts while taking [insert antidepressant here] and drinking. Prozac, specifically had over 500 documenting cases of blacking out on one webpage alone (Treato 2016).

Among the list of medications that popped up with significant references to black outs;
- Prozac
- Lamictal
- Zoloft
- Wellbutrin
- Lyrica
- Effexor

"As a criminal defense attorney, I see hundreds of clients annually who obtain medications from their physician for anxiety, sleep disorders or depression, yet are not warned to consume NO ALCOHOL when taking these medications. The synergistic effects caused by combining ANY amount of alcohol and these drugs can be devastating for the patient who is surprised to find himself or herself in jail for DUI-DWI, or even vehicular homicide. Blackout, seizures or major amnesia episodes are common. Effexor is currently involved with three of my clients, with others using various common SSRIs and benzodiazepines" (Head 2016).

When I tried to find the link that this attorney put in the body of his post, it was broken. I searched the title of his post, "Failure to Warn About SSRIs and Alcohol" and still, nothing. This was a continually occurring them when I tried to access intriguing articles about what patients had experienced while taking certain prescriptions. The links were always broken or the page had been taken down completely.

This happenstance finding of drug-induced black outs led me into several topics that are truly mind-blowing, including the fact that Serotonin Syndrome actually causes blackouts. And, that blackouts happen in mentally ill people without any substances consumed at all.

The most shocking piece of information is that Serotonin plays a key role in alcohol craving, dependence and abuse. And although the studies I found were specific to alcohol (ethanol) craving and Serotonin, it seems pretty likely that it probably causes cravings for other mind-altering drugs as well. Serotonin flips on the addict switch in individuals who are already weakened by their diagnosed mental disorder. It has been found that a person with no history of alcoholism or history of alcoholism in their family, while taking a Serotonergic drug (any of the SSRISs) would be prone to craving alcohol. (See Appendix D.)

Appendix D

SSRIs, Alcohol, Alcoholism and Cravings

"Some of the most commonly prescribed antidepressants are called reuptake inhibitors. What's reuptake? It's the process in which neurotransmitters are naturally reabsorbed back into nerve cells in the brain after they are released to send messages between nerve cells. A reuptake inhibitor prevents this from happening. Instead of getting reabsorbed, the neurotransmitter stays -- at least temporarily -- in the gap between the nerves, called the synapse" (WebMD 2016).

SSRIs cause an in increase in the neurotransmitter Serotonin. Alcohol causes a short-lived influx of Serotonin. Serotonin Syndrome is caused by too much Serotonin building up in the body. Do you see where I am going here? Check out the conclusion of a study completed in 1997 regarding the role Serotonin plays in alcohol abuse:

"Serotonin's actions have been linked to alcohol's effects on the brain and to alcohol abuse. Alcoholics and experimental animals that consume large quantities of alcohol show evidence of differences in brain serotonin levels compared with non-alcoholics. Both short- and long-term alcohol exposure also affect the serotonin receptors that convert the chemical signal produced by serotonin into functional changes in the signal-receiving cell. Drugs that act on these receptors alter alcohol consumption in both humans and animals. Serotonin, along with other neurotransmitters, also may contribute to alcohol's intoxicating and re. warding effects, and abnormalities in the brain's serotonin system appear to play an important role in the brain processes underlying alcohol abuse" (DM 1997).

Alcohol increases serotonin levels in the short term and you are on a SSRI, it would only make sense that your Serotonin levels would skyrocket, sending you into Serotonin Syndrome, where you engage in risky behaviors and act manic. This is also why people would experience "blacking out." The overload send your nervous system into overdrive. Then, because of the way alcohol works, there is a dramatic drop in Serotonin levels, and you would suffer a dramatized hangover, one that, if you are already depressed, may cause you to take action when you would not have.

Then, I think it is fair to say, with such a dramatic different in Serotonin levels, and having hit ecstasy with Serotonin Syndrome, the drop in Serotonin levels, may not only, cause the person to reach for alcohol again to get back to where they were mentally, their body may physiologically crave the influx of Serotonin and subconsciously cause the person to look for alcohol.

Drug companies would never want drinking to be in the way of their sales, so they don't warn patients in regard to this phenomenon.

> "There is an alarming connection between alcoholism and the various prescription drugs that increase serotonin. The most popular of those drugs are: PROZAC, ZOLOFT, PAXIL, LUVOX, SERZONE, EFFEXOR...For seven years numerous reports have been made by reformed alcoholics (some for 15 years and longer) who are being "driven" to alcohol again after being prescribed one of these drugs. And many other patients who had no previous history of alcoholism have continued to report an "overwhelming compulsion" to drink while using these drugs..." (Tracy 1994).

Tracy references a scientific study performed in 1994 on a new antidepressant drug, Chlorophenylpiperazine[MCPP] that works with the neurotransmitter Serotonin.

> "m-Chlorophenylpiperazine produced ethanollike effects and alcohol craving in recently detoxified alcoholics....These data further implicate serotonergic systems in the discriminative properties of ethanol

and may indicate a serotonergic contribution to craving" (Krystal 1994).

Appendix E

Rx Fx: Prozac (Fluoxetine)
- SSRI
- Antidepressant that requires black box warning for and suicidality

Aside from the FDA black box warning regarding SSRI's and their connection to
"increased suicidality in children and adults up to age twenty-four" (FDA 2009), there is this terrifying concept: Serotonin Syndrome, the likes of which I seem to have experienced first-hand.

Thank god my mother strictly adhered to her motherly principles, making many phone calls to psychiatrists and GPs demanding that they immediately take me off of the drugs they had recklessly prescribed to her teenage daughter. I know now that she actually threatened to report the doctors if they didn't retract their advice for me to take those drugs.

Fortunately, I was under eighteen at the time. I was recklessly prescribed Prozac and my mother had the authority to drag me, unwillingly, into the doctor's that afternoon, barefoot and all. As I got older, the doctors refused to speak with her, explaining that I was eighteen and therefore, she was not privileged to the information on my charts.

You can imagine the distress, watching your completely normal child go completely nuts after being prescribed a drug to make her happier.

The correlation between my "seeing in color" and the addition of Prozac into my bloodstream is hardly random. What's worse? Based upon this reaction, to a very steep increase in the Prozac, I am diagnosed as bipolar and led onto a path of psychotropic drugs. This leads me into several life-threatening circumstances, most of which, if not all, are directly related to a new or shifting prescription.

The pharmaceutical industry took my entire teenage life and went forward to claim my college years as well. I was terrified now to find that there is actual evidence that this reaction, the Prozac-fueled pseudo manic episode that causes the bipolar diagnosis is common.

Below is a chunk from an article a psychiatric resident wrote regarding the strange phenomenon:

> "When I took my psychiatric residency at Harvard...in the early 1960s, we never saw or diagnosed bipolar disorder in children. In my four years of training, I saw one 19-year-old in a manic state and a few adults. When a person was admitted in a manic condition talking a mile a minute, imagining grand things about themselves, making outrageous plans, bursting with anger and energy, unable to sleep and otherwise euphoric, the condition was so unusual that we would hold grand rounds, a medical show-and-tell, to discuss the patient" (Breggin 2016).

Hang on, it gets even worse. Breggin continues:

> "Now psychiatric wards are filled with patients having their second and third or umpteenth manic episode and every psychiatrist's day is filled with patients diagnosed bipolar. It's mostly about antidepressant-induced mania" (Breggin 2016).

Did you read that closely? He said antidepressant-induced mania aka me!

> "Every single child I have evaluated who has suffered what looks like a manic episode has been taking stimulants or antidepressants, both of which cause mania. At least 9 out of 10 adults I've seen in the last two decades who have suffered emotional episodes that could be diagnosed as mania had them in direct response to stimulants or antidepressants–mostly the newer antidepressants starting with Prozac" (Breggin 2016).

Drops mic

And, although it would seem like a given, Prozac's FDA label clearly states what my prescribing psychiatrist, Dr. Jensen, didn't seem to understand when she started me on this powerful drug and then left for Africa.

> "Patients of all ages who are started on antidepressant therapy should be monitored appropriately and observed closely for clinical worsening, suicidality, or unusual changes in behavior. Families and caregivers should be advised of the need for close observation and communication with the prescriber" (FDA 2016).

Appendix F

Black Box Warning for Antiepileptic Drugs

Like their predecessors, the SSRIs, the anticonvulsants drugs all got slapped with a black box warning for suicidality after studies were consistent across the board on eleven different drugs that these medications produce suicidal thoughts and ideations.

> "AED class label changes :Manufacturers of antiepileptic drugs (AEDs) or anticonvulsant drugs will update product labeling to include a warning about an increased risk of suicidal thoughts or actions and will develop a Medication Guide to help patients understand this risk (FDA 2009).

The AEDs affected are listed below; (FDA 2009)
- Carbatrol
- Celontin
- Depakene
- Depakote ER
- Depakote sprinkles
- Depakote tablets
- Dilantin
- Equetro
- Felbatol
- Gabitril
- Keppra
- Keppra XR
- Klonopin
- Lamictal
- Lyrica
- Mysoline
- Neurontin
- Peganone S
- tavzor
- Tegretol
- Tegretol

- XR
- Topamax
- Tranxene
- Tridione
- Trileptal
- Zarontin
- Zonegran

Appendix G

Rx Fx: Wellbutrin (Bupropion Hydrochloride)

Antidepressant that requires black box warning for and suicidality
Dr. Morano wrote two words beside Wellbutrin on my chart: "jittery & nervous."
Dr. Fiaschetti wrote just one: "crabby."
Here is what part of the black box warning on this medication reads:

> "WARNING Suicidality and Antidepressant Drugs Use in Treating Psychiatric Disorders: Antidepressants increased the risk compared to placebo of suicidal thinking and behavior (suicidality) in children, adolescents, and young adults in short-term studies of major depressive disorder (MDD) and other psychiatric disorders. Anyone considering the use of WELLBUTRIN or any other antidepressant in a child, adolescent, or youngadult must balance this risk with the clinical need. Short-term studies did not show an increase in the risk of suicidality with antidepressants compared to placebo in adults beyond age 24..."(Gartlehner et. al. 2011).

The drug ZYBAN® contains the same active ingredients as Wellbutrin. But it is *not* indicated as a treatment for depression

> "WELLBUTRIN®,WELLBUTRIN SR® and WELLBUTRIN XL® are not approved for smoking cessation treatment, but bupropion under the name ZYBAN® is approved for this use" (Gartlehner et. al. 2011).

Confused? I am too. Wellbutrin, Wellbutrin SR, Wellbutrin XL and ZYBAN are all the same drug marketed differently.
One of the more frightening aspects of Wellbutrin, is what I found linking spells of blacking out directly with the use of Wellbutrin. On a site called Treato, you can vote if certain drugs caused certain

reactions. "Wellbutrin" and "blacking out" showed up in almost 500 posts. (Treato 2016)

I had to stop reading the posts because they are so frighteningly familiar. It turns out Wellbutrin blackouts are common. Dr. Morano never said anything to me about not drinking while taking Wellbutrin.

> "There are a number of reported cases of people losing consciousness and getting violent when combining Wellbutrin and alcohol, even after only a few drinks. This seems to be a normal occurrence and could spell disaster if you are in the wrong place when combining these two drugs" (SafetyMedical 2016).

Appendix H

Rx Fx: Lyrica (Pregabalin)
- AED that requires black box warning on suicidality
- Reported instances of blacking out while driving, no alcohol involved.

I liked Lyrica until it started making me super dizzy. However, it looks like my mother didn't. It's noted in the doctor's charts that I was "manic" while taking Lyrica. I think this was probably just my mom's opinion, but mothers do seem to know best.

Dr. Morano gave me Lyrica for the overall body aches I felt. These were probably partly due to injury and partly due to the chemical hell I was putting my body through, from stress alone. Lyrica's black box warning has to do with Lyrica and other anticonvulsant/antiepileptic drugs used to treat epileptic seizures (and in my case, general body aches...WTF?) and their link to an increase in suicidality just like their partners in crime, the SSRI's.

> "The FDA has completed its analysis of reports of suicidality...from placebo-controlled clinical trials of drugs used to treat epilepsy, psychiatric disorders, and other conditions. Based on the outcome of this review, FDA is requiring that all manufacturers of drugs in this class include a Warning in their labeling and develop a Medication Guide to be provided to patients prescribed these drugs to inform them of the risks of suicidal thoughts or actions" (FDA 2009).

It goes further, highlighting the exact same precautions from the SSRI label.

> "All patients who are currently taking or starting on any antiepileptic drug for any indication should be monitored for notable changes in behavior that could indicate the emergence or worsening of suicidal thoughts or behavior or depression" (FDA 2009).

The discussion boards in regard to Lyrica and blacking out are astounding. People agreed that blacking out is a common side effect, and on one page alone I read two stories involving car crashes due to experiencing a Lyrica black out while driving. With Lyrica, unlike the SSRI's, patients blacked out on Lyrica alone, there was no alcohol involved! (Medschat 2016).

Appendix I

Rx Fx Seroquel (Quetiapine Fumarate)
- Requires black box warning for and suicidality

Seroquel is an anti-psychotic drug that, in my circle alone, was taken by at least two people, including Jaxx's mother. Jaxx warned me about Seroquel because he'd watched his mother. He said it made her "fat."

I laughed it off until I remembered my mother's comment from the night prior regarding how much I'd been eating late at night.

"I've never seen you crave so much junk in my life!" she says as I shove multiple slices of sourdough bread topped with chunks of melted cheddar cheese into my mouth.

I wipe away the oil from my mouth to ask the age-old question, "Do you think I'm fat, Mom?" under a late-night haze of Seroquel zombie-ness. I could barely make out her facial features as my eyesight stayed in a constant "just woke up" blur on Seroquel.

Guess what?

AstraZeneca paid $647 million for a global lawsuit alleging that Seroquel caused diabetes… California will receive more than $5.2 million" (Wilson 2011).

How about that! It's even written in my medical charts that I craved sugar and carbohydrates late at night. It was prescribed to me to help with insomnia but looks like it's not even approved for this use. It is an anti-psychotic.

AstraZeneca paid another $68.5 million "as part of a multistate settlement over allegations that it promoted its psychiatric drug Seroquel for unapproved uses, such as treating insomnia and Alzheimer's disease" (Ceasar 2011). It is estimated that "AstraZeneca will have paid a total of about $1.9 billion to defend and settle the personal injury cases and government investigations. The figure represents less than five months of Seroquel sales" (Wilson 2011)

Appendix J

Rx Fx Lamictal (Lamotrigine)
- AED that requires black box on suicidality

Lamictal is another one of the antiepileptic medications carrying the black box warning regarding its effect and an increase in suicidality (FDA 2009). This is a trend throughout the path of drugs I am prescribed. Here's what the FDA website has to say:

> "As described on January 31, 2008, Information for Health Care Professionals Sheet on AEDS, eleven antiepileptic drugs were included in FDA's original pooled analysis of placebo-controlled clinical studies in which these drugs were used to treat epilepsy as well as psychiatric disorders and other conditions. The increased risk of suicidal thoughts or behavior was generally consistent among the eleven drugs...This observation suggests that the risk applies to all antiepileptic drugs used for any indication" (FDA 2009).

I hated Lamictal. It was like the Soma for doctors. If there were no solutions, they'd throw in Lamictal. I, however, had to suffer the consequences.

Dr. Fiaschetti's notes read: "at 125mg couldn't get out of bed."

Well, that doesn't work, now does it Doc?

I felt disconnected from my body on Lamictal: awkward, dizzy, ill. It did nothing for depression. If anything, it worsened depression because I felt so sick and looked so damn pale while taking it!

On Treato.com 375 people posted on Lamictal and blacking out. There are posts about waking up being raped, having no control of their body, and blacking out while driving. (Treato 2016).

Appendix K

Rx Fx Abilify (Aripiprazole)

The migraine that this little blue pill gave me was one I will not soon forget: a skull-crunching headache that lasted for hours.

I can remember studying the conveniently put together sample pack complete with a stylized cursive, squiggly "A" for Abilify and providing enough medicine for an entire week. It was vacuum-sealed on a path-like design, urging you to wake up the next day and punch out the next step forward on the path of doses of Abilify.

After the migraines subsided, the exhaustion set in. I couldn't even make it through a week of this med. Along with being a member of the increasing suicidality drug squad (Epocrates 2016), Abilify causes some pretty extraordinary things. The FDA released this statement:

> "The U.S. Food and Drug Administration (FDA) is warning that compulsive or uncontrollable urges to gamble, binge eat, shop, and have sex have been reported with the use of the antipsychotic drug aripiprazole..." (FDA 2016).

A label does not solve the problem The FDA explains that the compulsive behavior ceases when the medication is stopped and that these reactions surfaced in people who had no history of impulse control issues prior and who had no issues after stopping the drug.

> "In the majority of cases, patients with no prior history of the compulsive behaviors experienced uncontrollable urges only after starting aripiprazole treatment. Within days to weeks of reducing the dose or discontinuing aripiprazole, these uncontrollable urgesstopped" (FDA 2016).

And this side effect is especially relevant in my case. Compulsive would be the nicest way to put how I acted.

"A search of the FDA Adverse Event Reporting System (FAERS) database and the medical literature in the 13 years since the approval of the first aripiprazole product (Abilify) in November 2002 identified a total of 184 case reports in which there was an association between aripiprazole use and impulse-control problems" (FDA 2009).

This is frightening because this number reflects only the amount of cases that were reported to the FAERS. I've never even heard of FAERS and even if I had heard of it, there would be no way, at the time, that I'd actually take the time to call them up and explain that I felt this particular drug was the reason for my impulse-control issues. Especially as a young adult, you have to be extremely self-confident to, not only see a problem, but to take the time to locate its origin, and do so without blaming yourself. The fact that any cases are reported to this agency is suspect.

Appendix L

Rx Fx Geodon (Ziprasidone)

Dr. Fiaschetti's notes read: "Geodon—worked ok during the summer but in early classes at school, you saw triple. Made you hyper for the 1st three hours after you took it and then groggy all the next day."

In 2007, the FDA attacked Pfizer's Geodon for bad marketing. Pfizer ran an advertisement in a popular medical journal that, according to the FDA was, "'false or misleading because it omits important risk information and contains unsubstantiated superiority claims'" (Smith 2007). By taking out these risks, the FDA claims that Pfizer "misleadingly suggests that Geodon...is safer than has been demonstrated" (Smith 2007).

Here's some food for thought regarding how big of a business manipulating our mental health has become:

> "Geodon sales totaled $400 million in the first half of 2007, according to Pfizer. The drug competes with Johnson & Johnson's Risperdal and Invega, which totaled $2.3 billion insales during the first six months of 2007, as well as Eli Lilly & Co.'s Zyprexa, Bristol Myers Squibb's Abilify and AstraZeneca's Seroquel" (Smith 2007).

Appendix M

Rx Fx Zoloft (Sertraline)
- SSRI
- Antidepressant that requires black box warning for and suicidality

I wasn't too interested in researching this one because I didn't feel anything while I was taking it. Funny, though, there is a lawsuit for this exact thing. There is class action lawsuit against Pfizer suing them on the grounds of the misrepresented effectiveness of their $3 billion revenue source. Zoloft is allegedly little more effectiveness than a sugar pill (Hedlund 2016).

Pfizer launched a massive campaign to manipulate the general public into purchasing Zoloft. They even went to the extent of falsifying clinical trials and "ghostwriting" articles about its effectiveness (Hedlund 2016). Below are some of the particulars:

> "the only two studies that showed Zoloft had more of an effect than placebo was obtained through data manipulation...By means of 'ghostwritten' medical journal articles (written by Pfizer or companies hired by Pfizer) and hidden payments to prominent physicians (known as key opinion leaders), Pfizer has concealed its significant influence over Zoloft's manufactured image of apparent effectiveness" (Hedlund 2016).

And just as the cherry on top, Zoloft is a member of the antidepressant class has the same black box warning as Prozac regarding an increase in suicidality (FDA 2011). See the black box warning below:

> "Suicidality and Antidepressant Drugs: Antidepressants increased the risk compared to placebo of suicidal thinking and behavior (suicidality) in children, adolescents, and young adults in short-term studies of major depressive disorder (MDD) and other

psychiatric disorders. Anyone considering the use of [Insert established name] or any other antidepressant in a child, adolescent, or young adult must balance this risk with the clinical need" (FDA 2011

There were 550 posts regarding blacking out while taking Zoloft and drinking on Treato, another huge number for something that is not warned against. (Treato 2016).

Appendix N

Rx Fx Effexor (Venlafaxine)
- Antidepressant that requires black box warning for and suicidality

The second time I heard the phrase "brain shivers" was when I searched Effexor on the Internet. There are memes devoted to this exact thing. Brain shivers are real and very much recognized as stemming directly from Effexor withdrawal. Other names for the hell Effexor withdrawal put me through include; "brain zaps" "antidepressant withdrawal syndrome" (Warner et. al. 2006), and my personal favorite, "cranial zaps" (Cortes et. al. 2013).

Effexor causes an increase in suicidality as well. (FDA 2011) Below is the Effexor Warning Letter from the FDA to Wyeth Pharmaceuticals regarding false claims made by Wyeth regarding efficacy and dangers of Effexor:

> "FDA) has reviewed a professional journal ad submitted by Wyeth Pharmaceuticals Inc. (Wyeth) for Effexor XR®...The journal ad is misleading...makes unsubstantiated superiority claims, in addition to other unsubstantiated claims, and minimizes the risks associated with the use of Effexor XR...These violations ... suggest that Effexor XR is safer and more effective than has been demonstrated...Effexor XR use is associated with a number of serious risks...such as suicidality in young adults, anxiety and insomnia, activation of mania/hypomania" (FDA 2007).

Appendix O

Rx Fx: Trileptal (Oxcarbazepine)
- AED that requires black box on suicidality

It looks like we've got another shapeshifter here! Just check out this title: "Novartis Pharmaceuticals Corp. to Pay More Than $420 Million to Resolve Off-label Promotion and Kickback Allegations" (The United States Department of Justice" [DOJ] 2010)."

It turns out that the makers of Trileptal, Novartis, marketed Trileptal and five other drugs for; "treatments not approved by the FDA, including relieving psychiatric symptoms and pain. The false promotions led to false claims in federal health care plans" (Drugwatch 2015).

Novartis pled guilty, but that's not all. The DOJ accused them of also: "illegally paying doctors kickbacks in the form of speaker programs, advisory boards, entertainment, travel, and meals to prescribe Trileptal to their patients" (Rottenstein Law Group [RLG] 2011).

On top of those allegations, there is nearly double the risk of suicidal ideation and suicide while taking this antiepileptic drug (RLG 2011). The FDA did a study on almost 50,000 people:

> "Of those on the antiepileptics, 0.43 percent experienced suicidal ideations. That's compared to the 0.22 percent of those who experienced suicidal thinking on the placebos...Four people taking the drugs did commit suicide; none of the placebo-takers did" (RLG 2011).

However, the FDA decided not to enforce a black box warning but rather had Novartis develop a "medication guide" (RLG 2011). Therefore, Novartis can continue marketing to the consumer without accurately identifying Trileptal or issuing appropriate safety warnings.

Appendix P

Rx Fx: Lithobid (Lithium)

The FDA did place a black box warning on Lithobid:

> "Lithium toxicity is closely related to serum lithium levels and can occur at doses close to therapeutic levels. Facilities for prompt and accurate serum lithium determination should be available before initiating therapy" (FDA 2016).

This medication reminded me of Lamictal. I didn't feel right while taking it. But all of the doctors favored it. Lithium is a natural element that one can find on our periodic table, and it's been used to treat bipolar disorder forever. Nonetheless, I hated every molecule of it. My eyesight got blurry. I was shaky, and my balance was so off that I couldn't turn in dance class. All of the adverse effects with regard to lithium boil down to lithium toxicity; a condition where your body is overwhelmed by an influx of lithium.

Some of the symptoms include; "drowsiness, muscular weakness and lack of coordination…At higher levels, giddiness, ataxia, blurred vision…" (Drugs.com: 2016). I experienced all of these things as well as several symptoms of acute lithium toxicity. I was even in the emergency room vomiting up blood.

Almost of the symptoms under "acute toxicity" appear in my case; "hand tremors, lack of coordination in arms and legs, muscle twitches," (Medline Plus 2016) as well as some of the "chronic toxicity" symptoms including; "uncontrolled shaking (tremors) memory problems, and movement disorders" (Medline 2016).

Appendix Q

Rx Fx: Topamax (Topiramate)

AED that requires black box on suicidality

Topamax is a member of the antiepileptic class of drugs that causes an increase in suicidality (FDA 2009). To top it all off:

> "The manufacturer, two subsidiaries of health care giant Johnson & Johnson, were found guilty of marketing the drug [Topamax] for unapproved treatments, such as weight loss and bipolar disorder. The Department of Justice fined Ortho-McNeil Pharmaceutical and Ortho- McNeil-Janssen Pharmaceuticals more than $81 million in 2010 for this dangerous practice" (Drugwatch 2016).

Appendix R

Rx Fx: Xanax (Alprazolam)

I found the black box warning labeled "Use with Other CNS Depressants" particularly frightening:

> "The benzodiazepines, including alprazolam (Xanax) produce additive CNS depressant effects when co-administered with other psychotropic med-ications, anticonvulsants, antihistaminics, ethanol and other drugs which themselves produce CNS de-pression" (Drugs.com 2016).

Appendix S

Rx Fx: Opioids (Vicodin (Acetaminophen/Hydrocodone), Norco (Acetaminophen/Hydrocodone), Roxicodone (Oxycodone), Oxycontin (Oxycodone), Subutex/Suboxone (Buprenorphine)

I always said that these opioid painkillers were an intelligent band of beasts. They attack the brain where it's most vulnerable and with the most addictive qualities. Their name states their effect, but it's bigger than just the physical. They have a physically addictive quality, but they also play mind games with you.

They leave you longing for their familiar haze, years after you've quit. I heard once from a doctor that opiate addiction is the only addiction that stays with you for a lifetime and I completely believe it. I can still taste the chewed-up Norco and the difference in taste when Jaxx switched to Roxis.

They didn't just kill the physical pain. They took the bite out of the everyday. They glossed over the daily redundancies of life. They put a clear, glossy coating over the nails you so carefully painted.

Vicodin

Vicodin is like a vodka soda, watered down by the ice melting in a steamy club. They were the pills that were stolen from parents' drug cabinets.

Norco

This has more hydrocodone than Vicodin, but also contains Acetaminophen, Vicodin is child's play in comparison to Norco.

Roxis

I came to find out that Roxicodone is just a brand name for Oxycodone, which is the same thing as Oxycontin.

Oxy

80's was the slang term for Oxycontin, which is Oxycodone. No one liked using their actual name, too much bad press, it scared people to say Oxycontin. For the longest time, nobody touched the drug Oxycontin.

Subutex

I was taking 80s of Oxycontin while trying to rid myself of the addiction via Subutex and subsequently got addicted to the Subutex, which was given out by my boyfriend, Jaxx, who was going through the same thing only worse.

Glossary of Useful Terms

AED:
Antiepileptic drug

Black Box Warning:
A warning placed on a prescription drug label that is encased in a black box outline to call attention to "serious or life-threatening risks" (FDA 2016).

Serotonin Syndrome (SS):
A life-threatening condition caused by having too much Serotonin, in the body (AAFM 2010).

> "This syndrome consists of a combination of mental status changes, neuromuscular hyperactivity, and autonomic hyperactivity. Serotonin syndrome can occur via the therapeutic use of serotonergic drugs alone, an intentional overdose of serotonergic drugs, or classically, as a result of a complex drug interac-tion between two serotonergic drugs that work by dif-ferent mechanisms" (Volpi-Abadi et. al. 2013).

SSRI:
Selective Serotonin Reuptake Inhibitors (Ferguson 2001), a type of antidepressant that works with the neurotransmitter Serotonin, e.g. Prozac.

Suicidality:
Likelihood of an individual to commit suicide (The Free Dictionary 2016).

References

Baum Hedlund. "Zoloft Class Action Claims Drug Company Misled Consumers About Zoloft's Ability To Treat Depression - Baum Hedlund". 2016. *Baum Hedlund*. https://www.baumhedlundlaw.com/consumer-class-actions/zoloft-class-action-claims-drug-company-misled-consumers-about-zolofts-ability-to-treat-depression/.

Breggin, Dr. Peter. 2016. "Making A Market In Antipsychotic Drugs: A Tragedy". *The Huffington Post*. http://www.huffingtonpost.com/dr-peter-breggin/making-a-market-in-antips_b_720861.html.

Ceasar, Stephen. "Astrazeneca To Pay $68.5 Million In Seroquel Settlement". 2011. *Latimes*. http://articles.latimes.com/2011/mar/11/business/la-fi-0311-astrazeneca-settlement-20110311.

CNN.Com. "FDA Accuses Pfizer Of False Advertising For Geodon - Aug. 13, 2007". 2016. *Money.CNN.Com*. http://money.cnn.com/2007/08/13/news/companies/geodon/.

Cortes, Jose A. and Rajiv Radhakrishnan. 2013. "A Case Of Amelioration Of Venlafaxine-Discontinuation "Brain Shivers" With Atomoxetine". *The Primary Care Companion For CNS Disorders*. doi:10.4088/pcc.12l01427.

Dick, Kirby. *The Hunting Ground*. 2015. Film. Directed By Kirby Dick. Los Angeles: The Weinstein Company.

DM, Lovinger. 2016. "Serotonin's Role In Alcohol's Effects On The Brain. - Pubmed - NCBI". *Ncbi.Nlm.Nih.Gov*. https://www.ncbi.nlm.nih.gov/pubmed/15704346.

Drobny, Shelby. 2016. "What Drug Companies Are Not Reporting About Alcohol And Anti-Depressants". *The Huffington Post*. http://www.huffingtonpost.com/sheldon-drobny/what-drug-companies-are-n_b_18063.html.

Drugs.com. "Ativan: Indications, Side Effects, Warnings - Drugs.Com". 2016. *Drugs.Com*. https://www.drugs.com/cdi/ativan.html.

Drugs.com. "Lithium - FDA Prescribing Information, Side Effects And Uses". 2016. *Drugs.Com*. https://www.drugs.com/pro/lithium.html.

Drugs.Com. "Xanax XR - FDA Prescribing Information, Side Effects And Uses". 2016. *Drugs.Com*. https://www.drugs.com/pro/xanax-xr.html#PRECdi.

Drugwatch. "Prescription Drug Settlement – Litigation For Dangerous Medication". 2016. *Drugwatch*. https://www.drugwatch.com/prescription-drug-settlements/.

Epocrates. "Abilify Black Box Warnings". 2016. *Epocrates*. https://online.epocrates.com/drugs/325811/Abilify/Black-Box-Warnings.

Ferguson, James. 2016. "SSRI Antidepressant Medications: Adverse Effects And Tolerability". *PubMed Central [PMC]*. https://www.ncbi.nlm.nih.gov/pmc/articles/PMC181155/.

Food and Drug Administration [FDA]. "Suicidal Behavior And Ideation And Antiepileptic Drugs". 2016. *Fda.Gov*. http://www.fda.gov/Drugs/DrugSafety/PostmarketDrugSafetyInformationforPatientsandProviders/ucm100190.htm.

Food and Drug Administration [FDA]. "A Guide To Safety Terms At The FDA". 2016. *FDA.Gov*. http://www.fda.gov/downloads/ForConsumers/ConsumerUpdates/UCM107976.pdf.

Food and Drug Administration [FDA]. "Antidepressant Use In Children, Adolescents, And Adults". 2016. *Fda.Gov*. http://www.fda.gov/Drugs/DrugSafety/InformationbyDrugClass/ucm096273.htm.

Food and Drug Administration [FDA]. "Aripiprazole (Abilify, Abilify Maintena, Aristada): Drug Safety Communication - FDA Warns About New Impulse-Control Problems". 2016.

*FDA.Gov.*http://www.fda.gov/Safety/MedWatch/SafetyInformation/SafetyAlertsforHumanMedicalProducts/ucm498823.htm.

Food and Drug Administration [FDA]. "FDA Drug Safety Communication: FDA Warns About New Impulse-Control Problems Associated With Mental Health Drug Aripiprazole (Abilify, Abilify Maintena, Aristada)". 2016. 1st ed. *FDA.Gov* http://www.fda.gov/downloads/drugs/drugsafety/ucm498825.pdf.

Food and Drug Administration [FDA]. "Lithium". 2016. 1st ed. *FDA.Gov* http://www.accessdata.fda.gov/drugsatfda_docs/label/2002/18027s40s46s49lbl.pdf.

Food and Drug Administration [FDA]. "Soma (Carisoprodol)". 2016. *Fda.Gov.* http://www.fda.gov/Safety/MedWatch/SafetyInformation/ucm191961.htm.

Food and Drug Administration [FDA]. 2016. "Effexor Warning Letter". FDA.Gov. http://www.fda.gov/downloads/Drugs/GuidanceComplianceRegulatoryInformation/EnforcementActivitiesbyFDA/WarningLettersandNoticeofViolationLetterstoPharmaceuticalCompanies/ucm054126.pdf

Gartlehner, Gerald, Richard Hansen, Ursula Reichenpfader, Angela Kaminski, Christina Kien, Michaela Strobelberger, Megan Noord, Patricia Thieda, Kylie Thaler, and Bradley Gaynes. 2011. "Black Box Warnings Of Drugs Approved By The US Food And Drug Administration". *National Center for Biotechnology Information [NCBI].* http://www.ncbi.nlm.nih.gov/books/NBK54348/.

Head, William C. 2016. "Failure To Warn About Ssris & Alcohol". Drugs.Com. https://www.drugs.com/forum/latest-drug-related-news/failure-warn-about-ssris-alcohol-22715.html.

Jacqueline Volpi-Abadie, Alan David Kaye. 2016. "Serotonin Syndrome". PubMed Central [PMC]. https://www.ncbi.nlm.nih.gov/pmc/articles/PMC3865832/.

Justice.Gov. "Novartis Pharmaceuticals Corp. To Pay More Than $420 Million To Resolve Off-Label Promotion And Kickback Allegations". 2016. *Justice.Gov*. https://www.justice.gov/opa/pr/novartis-pharmaceuticals-corp-pay-more-420-million-resolve-label-promotion-and-kickback.

Krystal JH, et al. 2016. "Specificity Of Ethanollike Effects Elicited By Serotonergic And Noradrenergic Mechanisms. - Pubmed - NCBI". *Ncbi.Nlm.Nih.Gov*. https://www.ncbi.nlm.nih.gov/pubmed/7944878.

Medchat.com. "Memory Blackouts??? - Medschat". 2016. *Medschat.Com*. http://www.medschat.com/Discuss/Memory-Blackouts-178282.htm.

Medshadow. "Drug Classifications, Schedule I, II, III, IV, V - Medshadow". 2016. *Medshadow*. http://medshadow.org/drug-classifications-schedule-ii-iii-iv-v/.

New Life Outlook. ""Causes And Treatments Of Bipolar Blackouts". 2016. *Newlifeoutlook | Bipolar*. http://bipolar.newlifeoutlook.com/bipolar-blackouts/2/.

Perry, Dana. *Boy Interrupted*. 2009. Film. Directed by Dana Heinz Perry. HBO Films.

Rachal, Christopher. 2016. "Antidepressant Discontinuation Syndrome - American Family Physician". *Aafp.Org*. http://www.aafp.org/afp/2006/0801/p449.html.

Rottenstein Law Group. "Trileptal Injury Lawsuit : Rottenstein Law Group LLP". February 27, 2016. *Rotlaw.Com*. http://www.rotlaw.com/trileptal/.

SafetyMedical.Net. "Wellbutrin And Alcohol – Safety Medical". *Safetymedical.Net*. http://www.safetymedical.net/wellbutrin-and-alcohol.

Ssri.Stories. "9 Out Of 10 Bipolars Became This Way Through Antidepressant Induced Mania: Doctor Speaks | SSRI Stories". 2016. Ssristories.Org. https://ssristories.org/9-out-of-10-bipolars-became-this-way-through-antidepressant-induced-mania-doctor-speaks/.

The American Academy of Family Physicians [AAFP]. "Prevention, Diagnosis, And Management Of Serotonin Syndrome". 2016. *Aafp.Org*. http://www.aafp.org/afp/2010/0501/p1139.pdf.

The Free Dictionary. "Suicidality". 2016. *Thefreedictionary.Com*. http://medical-dictionary.thefreedictionary.com/Suicidality.

The Physicians Desk Reference [PDR]. "Ativan Tablets (Lorazepam) Dose, Indications, Adverse Effects, Interactions… ". 2016. *PDR.Net*. http://www.pdr.net/drug-summary/Ativan-Tablets-lorazepam-2135.

Tracy, Ann Blake. 2016. "ICFDA Alcohol Cravings Induced Via Serotonin". *Icfda.Drugawareness.Org*. http://icfda.drugawareness.org/Archives/Miscellaneous/MRalcohol.html.

Treato.com "Can Lamictal Cause Blackouts?". 2016. *Treato*. https://treato.com/Blackouts,Lamictal/?a=s.

Treato.com "Can Zoloft Cause Blackouts?". 2016. *Treato*. https://treato.com/Blackouts,Zoloft/?a=s.

Treato.com. "Can Wellbutrin Cause Blackouts?". 2016. *Treato*. https://treato.com/Wellbutrin,Blackouts/?a=s#!.

WebMD. "How Different Antidepressants Work". 2016. *Webmd*. http://www.webmd.com/depression/how-different-antidepressants-work#1.

Welch, Brian J., Dion Graybeal, Orson W. Moe, Naim M. Maalouf, and Khashayar Sakhaee. 2006. "Biochemical And Stone-Risk Profiles With Topiramate Treatment". *American Journal Of Kidney Diseases* 48 (4): 555-563. doi:10.1053/j.ajkd.2006.07.003.

Wilson, Duff. 2016. "Astrazeneca Settles Most Seroquel Suits". *Prescriptions Blog*.

http://prescriptions.blogs.nytimes.com/2011/07/28/astrazeneca-settles-most-seroquel-suits/?_r=1.

Thank You

If you enjoyed the book, please share it with your friends! I very much appreciate your support.

Follow me
for updates, giveaways, inspirational posts, and exciting events to come & the updated release dates for the next books in the
Finding Kali Trilogy!

Twitter: @kaliraewheeler

Instagram: @kaliraewheeler

Blog: kaliraewheeler.com

Do you want to get involved?
Have you been through similar experiences?
Please share!
Help me start the discussion on social media with
#losingkali or #findingkalitriology

I'd love to hear your story.
Or
let's get personal!

Visit kaliraewheeler.com
Click "Connect" & send me a message!

Love and Light <3

Namaste,
Kali Rae Wheeler

www.ingramcontent.com/pod-product-compliance
Lightning Source LLC
Chambersburg PA
CBHW060514080526
44586CB00012B/480